WEST'S LAW SCHOOL ADVISORY BOARD

CIVIL PROCE-DURE

IN A NUTSHELL

FOURTH EDITION

By

MARY KAY KANE

Dean and Professor of Law, University of California,
Hastings College of the Law

ST. PAUL, MINN.
WEST PUBLISHING CO.
1996

Library of Congress Cataloging-in-Publication Data

ISBN 0–314–06641–1

 TEXT IS PRINTED ON 10% POST CONSUMER RECYCLED PAPER

 Printed with Printwise Environmentally Advanced Water Washable Ink

PREFACE

This edition follows the same format and approach of those that preceded it. The primary revisions have been to update the work in light of some very important legislative, rulemaking, and judicial developments that have occurred since the Third Edition was published in 1991.

Congress has revised several of the federal jurisdiction statutes. Most striking is its adoption of a supplemental jurisdiction statute, replacing the judicial doctrines of ancillary and pendent jurisdiction, as well as changes to removal jurisdiction. These enactments clarify some issues about which the courts have been divided, but also raise new interpretation questions that will need to be resolved.

On the rulemaking front, the Supreme Court has issued several amendments to the federal rules of civil procedure in the last five years. These amendments have resulted in entirely new service of process provisions, a significant change in the attorney signature requirement for pleadings and other papers, and the adoption of a new mandatory disclosure scheme as part of the discovery process. Thus, these changes require some serious assessment in civil procedure courses and this edition has been rewritten to provide at least an introduction to the issues that are presented under these new provisions.

Finally, as was true in the Third Edition, in addition to updating, In have tried to make some adjustments to provide clearer explanations of some topics. In hope that these changes will make the book more helpful to the student reader.

The overall objective of this book remains an important, but limited, one—to present the forest instead of the trees. There is no way in the confines of these few pages that more in depth coverage could be achieved. Readers who find a need for more can consult my Hornbook on this same topic, J. Friedenthal, M. Kane & A. Miller, *Civil Procedure* (2d ed.1993).

MARY KAY KANE

San Francisco, California
January, 1996

OUTLINE

OUTLINE

OUTLINE

Page

*

TABLE OF CASES

References are to Pages

TABLE OF CASES

TABLE OF CASES

*

TABLE OF STATUTES

UNITED STATES

UNITED STATES CONSTITUTION

UNITED STATES CODE ANNOTATED
15 U.S.C.A.—Commerce and Trade

TABLE OF STATUTES

TABLE OF STATUTES

ILLINOIS SMITH–HURD ANNOTATED

MICHIGAN GENERAL COURT RULES

MINNESOTA RULES OF CIVIL PROCEDURE

MINNESOTA RULES OF CIVIL APPELLATE PROCEDURE

NEW YORK, MCKINNEY'S CIVIL PRACTICE LAW AND RULES

NORTH CAROLINA GENERAL STATUTES

TABLE OF STATUTES

RHODE ISLAND GENERAL LAWS

*

TABLE OF RULES

FEDERAL RULES OF CIVIL PROCEDURE

TABLE OF RULES

FEDERAL RULES OF CIVIL PROCEDURE

TABLE OF RULES

FEDERAL RULES OF CIVIL PROCEDURE

FEDERAL RULES OF EVIDENCE

*

CIVIL PROCEDURE

IN A NUTSHELL

FOURTH EDITION

*

CHAPTER I

INTRODUCTION

§ 1–1. General Background

The basic first year civil procedure course is designed to teach how lawyers choose a proper court and how they frame and present their cases throughout the proceedings until a judgment has been reached and all available appeals have been pursued. The effect of judgments on future litigation also may be explored. Thus, the primary focus in this book is on the methods and tools available to lawyers as litigators. This study requires an inquiry into judicially developed doctrines, as well as various rules and statutes governing the operation and process of the civil courts. At times it will produce questions that are theoretical or constitutional; at other times issues of careful or strict rule interpretation will be paramount. Throughout, it is important to keep in mind the purpose underlying the development of civil procedure rules and doctrine—to provide a just, efficient, and economical means by which parties can resolve their disputes. Not always will this purpose be met and, indeed, some of the existing procedures have been used by attorneys to thwart this goal. Nonetheless, the desire to achieve justice, efficiency, and economy in our civil dispute resolution process underlies the way in which the courts apply and interpret the governing rules.

In studying the procedures by which legal rights are vindicated, it also is important to note that the Anglo–American judicial system is based on the adversary model. The judge sits solely to rule on disputed questions, as presented by the parties, and to apply sanctions when they are properly requested by a party. The lawyers shape the contours of the action. Issues not raised, objections not made, or points not challenged are, with very few exceptions, waived. The case moves forward only in response to the demands of the parties. Although judges in recent times have tended to take a somewhat more active role in guiding the litigation before them, it still remains true that the ultimate responsibility for each case rests with the litigants and their attorneys.

Finally, it should be noted that there is a very important aspect to framing litigation that typically is not taught in the basic civil procedure course and will not b discussed in this book: how to select a particular remedy as the one most likely to succeed or best suited to the needs of the client. That inquiry concerns matters such as whether injunctive relief or damages may be sought or whether some form of restitutionary relief might be most appropriate. Historically, the question of what type of relief was involved also dictated the court in which suit should be filed. This was because there were separate courts established—i.e., law, equity, ecclesiastical—to dispense certain types of relief or to hear certain types of disputes. Modern court systems are not so designed. Instead, any civil court is authorized to dispense whatever remedy is appropriate. Thus, the problem of framing a remedy, while an essential step in preparing your case, is not particularly relevant in the selection of a court and is left to a course in remedies. An excellent treatment of that problem may be found in D. Dobbs, *Remedies* (2d ed.1993).

§ 1–2. Current Structure of Court Systems

There are fifty-two separate court systems in the United States. Each state, as well as the District of Columbia, has its own fully developed, independent system of courts and there is a separate federal court system. The federal courts are not superior to the state courts; they are an independent, coordinate system authorized by the United States Constitution, Art. III, § 2, to handle matters of particular federal interest. The presence of two parallel court systems often raises questions concerning the relationship of the state and federal systems, presenting important issues of federalism. See §§ 9–2—9–5, below. The United States Supreme Court, composed of nine justices, sits as the final and controlling voice over all these systems.

Although a few states, such as Nebraska, have a two-tiered system, most states, as well as the federal courts, are based on a three-tiered model. That means that for any litigant there will be the opportunity to present his case in a trial court and then, should he lose, there are two levels of appeal at which the losing trial litigant ultimately may succeed. For example, in the federal system the trial court is the United States District Court, of which there is at least one in every state. Many larger states are divided into two, three or even four judicial districts, depending on population, geography and caseload. There are ninety-one districts in the United States and each district court has one judge, or more commonly two or more. After an adverse judgment in the district court, a litigant may appeal to the United States Court of Appeals for the circuit in which the district court is located. There are eleven numbered intermediate appellate courts in the federal system, each including anywhere from three to ten states and territories. Additionally, there is a Court of Appeals for the District of Columbia, hearing appeals from the federal district court there, and one for the Federal Circuit, taking appeals from various specialized federal tribunals, such as the Claims Court. Each court of appeals has four or more judges who sit in panels of three to review district court decisions, as well as some decisions of administrative agencies. A losing litigant in the court of appeals may, in some cases, be able to obtain review by the United States Supreme Court. Cases in the state courts similarly may proceed through a trial court, a state appellate court, and then the state supreme court. If a federal constitutional question is involved, the decision of the state supreme court may be reviewed by the United States Supreme Court. Since 1988, review by the Supreme Court in civil cases is discretionary; virtually all civil appeals as of right to the highest court have been abolished.

Three-tiered systems vary on the role which the highest court plays. The approaches taken reflect differing philosophies with regard to what the highest court should do. For example, in California only criminal cases in which capital punishment has been imposed are appealable as of right to the state supreme court. Similarly, in the federal courts, except in a few very limited circumstances, appeals to the United States Supreme Court are discretionary, by writ of certiorari. The Supreme Court decides for itself what are the most important questions that deserve its attention and will refuse to review decisions raising issues that it feels are not as crucial. In this way it supervises the administration of law by the lower courts on an ad hoc basis. At the other end of the spectrum, such as in New York, appeals to the state's highest court are as of right in a great many cases. This approach emphasizes the function of New York's highest court to assure that cases are correctly decided. Recognizing the wide disparity between judicial systems on this question, it is necessary to check carefully the statutes of the system in which suit is filed to determine the specific rules regarding review by those appellate courts.

CHAPTER II

CHOOSING THE PROPER COURT

A. SUBJECT–MATTER JURISDICTION

1. IN GENERAL

§ 2–1. Principles Governing

The first question that must be addressed when deciding where to file suit is which courts have the requisite power or competence to decide the type of controversy involved. This requirement typically is stated in terms of whether the court has subject-matter jurisdiction. Questions of subject-matter jurisdiction are determined by referring to federal and state statutes, which authorize jurisdiction over particular types of cases.

For state courts typically the statutes establishing the different courts in the state will set each court's subject-matter jurisdiction boundaries. State subject-matter jurisdiction limits exist primarily as a means of regulating the flow of judicial business before the state courts. In some instances jurisdiction will be distributed according to the type of proceeding involved, as in the case of probate proceedings or criminal matters. Amount restrictions also may serve to delineate court boundaries. For example, matters involving less than $10,000 may be assigned to Municipal Court, while matters involving more than that amount will be heard by the Superior Court. Few problems arise in applying these limitations. The question is not whether the plaintiff can bring an action in state court, but which of the existing state courts is authorized to hear the case.

The approach changes when federal subject-matter jurisdiction is involved. Federal courts are courts of *general* jurisdiction. That is to say, all federal district courts are treated as trial courts of equal jurisdictional power; there is no division among the district courts as to what cases can be tried in which tribunal. A federal district court may entertain an action based on almost any area of the law. The one exception to this principle is the existence of specialized federal courts to handle certain matters, such as the Tax Court, the Claims Court and the Bankruptcy Court. However, even in those cases the plaintiff may have the option of filing suit in the specialized federal court or in the federal district court.

The problem in defining federal court subject-matter jurisdiction arises because Article III, Section 2 of the U.S. Constitution limits federal jurisdiction solely to those matters specifically listed in that clause. All other controversies are left to the state courts to decide. Further, Article III delegates to the Congress the task of deciding what federal lower courts to establish. The Congress in enacting enabling legislation for the judicial power clause is under no obligation to give the federal courts all the jurisdiction authorized under the Constitution and in some instances it has refrained from doing so. As a result, the plaintiff who wants to file an action in federal court is not confronted with the issue of which federal court to file suit in so as to obtain subject-matter jurisdiction, but whether any federal court can entertain the controversy at all.

There may be a number of reasons why a plaintiff may prefer a federal forum. The applicable rules governing the procedures to be followed during the trial may be more liberal than the state rules. The federal court may be more conveniently located than the nearest state court. Federal judges often are perceived as having more expertise than their state counterparts. Further, they may be subject to fewer outside pressures because they are not elected but are appointed for life. Whatever the reason, federal subject-matter jurisdiction is strictly limited. In order to use the federal courts as a forum, the plaintiff must determine whether the federal courts have been given *concurrent* jurisdiction with the states over the particular controversy. This inquiry may present a complex constitutional, as well as a statutory, problem and it often has been the subject of litigation.

Before turning to an examination of federal subject-matter jurisdiction, a distinction must be drawn between *original* and *appellate* jurisdiction. Courts having original jurisdiction are courts of first instance—that is where to go to obtain a trial of the case. Courts having appellate jurisdiction function as reviewing courts and the case may be brought to them only on appeal from an order or judgment in a lower court. Thus, any inquiry into subject-matter jurisdiction must consider not only whether the court has been given the power to hear a certain controversy, but also whether it is a trial or an appellate tribunal.

In a few instances the jurisdiction statute will give a particular court *exclusive* jurisdiction over a particular type of controversy so that only that court will be a proper forum. For example, the federal courts have been given exclusive jurisdiction over actions based on patents and copyrights (28 U.S.C.A. § 1338), and over all proceedings in bankruptcy (28 U.S.C.A. § 1334) and no action on those matters can be brought in the state courts. Conversely, probate and divorce actions are within the exclusive jurisdiction of the state courts and, in most instances only properly brought before certain specialized state courts established to handle those cases. Interestingly, the exclusive jurisdiction of state probate and family courts is not of statutory origin. It is an historic division of authority that the state and federal courts have continued to recognize, although not required to do so as a matter of statutory or constitutional law.

A brief introduction to the main types of general federal jurisdiction and its restraints follows. Readers interested in a more detailed review should refer to J. Friedenthal, M. Kane & A. Miller, *Civil Proce-*

dure §§ 2.1—2.14 (2d ed.1993), or C. Wright, *Federal Courts* 100–255 (5th ed.1994).

2. FEDERAL JURISDICTION

§ 2–2. Federal Question Jurisdiction

The Constitution provides for federal court jurisdiction whenever a case "arises under" federal law. Many federal statutes create the right to sue for the violation of the rights or duties enumerated therein (e.g., federal antitrust or securities laws), and at the same time explicitly grant jurisdiction to the federal courts to hear those matters. In this way *special federal question jurisdiction* is established. The Congress also has provided in 28 U.S.C.A. § 1331, that the federal courts may take jurisdiction over any civil action arising under the Constitution, laws or treaties of the United States. The chief problem in invoking this *general federal question jurisdiction* has been in determining how to apply the "arising under" requirement in the statute. Stated most simply, a right or immunity created by federal law must be a basic element of the plaintiff's cause of action, not merely a collateral issue or introduced by way of defense. Gully v. First Nat. Bank in Meridian (S.Ct.1936).

The notion that a case does not "arise under" federal law if the defendant, rather than the plaintiff, introduces the federal issue was established by the United States Supreme Court in Louisville & Nashville R. Co. v. Mottley (S.Ct.1908). No language in the Constitution mandates that interpretation. Indeed, the Court has interpreted the constitutional language much more liberally, holding that as long as a federal question is an "original ingredient" in the case, even if it does not present an issue to be litigated, the Constitution may be satisfied. Osborn v. Bank of the United States (S.Ct.1824). Nonetheless, it has firmly embraced the "well-pleaded complaint" rule on numerous occasions as the appropriate interpretation of Congressional intent in using the "arising under" language in Section 1331.

Federal court jurisdiction can be invoked under that statute only when the statement of the plaintiff's claim, properly pleaded, shows that it is based on federal law. Emphasis is placed on what are the proper and necessary elements of a claim for relief. Jurisdiction is not proper if the plaintiff improperly anticipates a defense or if it is based on the defendant's counterclaim. Although the well-pleaded complaint rule has been criticized because it makes jurisdiction turn on technical pleading rules when rigid pleading no longer is part of federal procedure (see § 3–4, below), it remains the governing principle in federal question cases under Section 1331. Further, it has been extended to declaratory judgment actions, requiring an inquiry in those suits as to how the action would have been pleaded but for the availability of declaratory relief. As a practical matter this means that federal question jurisdiction will exist only if the coercive or damage action that would have been brought if the declaratory judgment remedy did not exist would have satisfied the well-pleaded complaint rule. Skelly Oil Co. v. Phillips Petroleum Co. (S.Ct.1950).

§ 2–3. Diversity of Citizenship Jurisdiction

Article III, Section 2 of the Constitution provides for jurisdiction over cases involving citizens of different states. In addition, the enabling statute provides for diversity jurisdiction in suits between citizens of a state and foreign citizens (aliens), 28 U.S.C.A. § 1332(a)(2), (3). All diversity jurisdiction is limited in the statute to disputes involving more than $50,000 (see § 2–4, below), however. No federal jurisdiction is provided for actions between two aliens or when one of the parties is a United States citizen but has no state citizenship. State courts are the only available fora in those cases. A further restriction on the invocation of federal diversity jurisdiction is the interpretation of the statute given by the Supreme Court in Strawbridge v. Curtiss (S.Ct.1806). The Court ruled that there must be complete diversity; in multi-party suits no plaintiff can share the same state citizenship with any defendant.

State citizenship is determined on the basis of a party's domicile, as opposed to mere residence. A person will be found to be domiciled in a state if she maintains her principal establishment there. Domicile requires the physical presence of a residence within the state plus the intention to make that residence one's present home. It is not required that the party whose domicile is in issue intend to reside there permanently. Persons such as servicemen, prisoners, and students can establish a domicile even though they may be only involuntarily or temporarily residing in a state. The key is whether they intend to maintain their principal establishment there for the time being. Once established, a domicile continues unless and until a new one is acquired.

The application of diversity requirements to actions involving business entities provides some problems. In the case of corporations, the diversity statute provides for citizenship both where the corporation is incorporated and where it maintains its principal place of business. 28 U.S.C.A. § 1332(c)(1). In many instances, this provision reduces the availability of diversity jurisdiction because a corporation is deemed a citizen of two states. A major difficulty in applying the statutory criteria is in deciding what constitutes a principal place of business. Most courts look to the site of the major production or service activities of the corporation, although others look to the location of the corporate headquarters, at least when the corporate operations are divided among several states. With unincorporated associations, such as labor unions, there are no special statutory guidelines, so the diversity statute has been interpreted to require an inquiry into the citizenship of all the members of the association. If any of the members are domiciled in the same state as the opponent, there is no complete diversity. United Steelworkers of America, AFL–CIO v. R.H. Bouligny, Inc. (S.Ct.1965).

Whether diversity of citizenship exists is determined as of the time the action is commenced. The citizenship of the parties at the time the cause of action arose or during the later course of the proceedings is not determinative. Thus, the plaintiff can change domiciles just before filing suit in order to create diversity. In some cases diversity has been artificially created by the plaintiff appointing an out-of-state representative or assigning his claim to a party diverse from the defendant. These tactics have been challenged on the ground that they violate the federal anticollusive jurisdiction statute, 28 U.S.C.A. § 1359. Assignments to create diversity have been struck down by the Supreme Court. See Kramer v. Caribbean Mills, Inc. (S.Ct.1969). However, most lower courts were reluctant to consider the motives behind the appointment of a representative in order to determine if Section 1359 had been violated. Thus, the Congress addressed the problem in 1988 when it amended the diversity statute to provide that the citizenship of legal representatives of estates or of infants or incompetents shall be deemed the same as the state of the decedent or the infant or incompetent being represented. 28 U.S.C.A. § 1332(c)(2). Consequently, there no longer is any incentive to appoint an out-of-state representative in order to fit within the diversity statute.

Diversity of citizenship jurisdiction has been under serious attack for several years. The historic premise for diversity was that it allowed entry into the federal courts in order to protect out-of-state residents from any potential prejudice that might exist in the local fora. There is serious question whether any modern justification for diversity exists and most commentators and courts agree that the historic rationale no longer presents a valid concern. With the caseload of the federal courts constantly increasing as new federal laws and claims are created, it is not surprising that several proposals have been made in the Congress to eliminate or seriously curtail diversity jurisdiction. To date, none have been successful, although the pressure for some restrictions continues.

§ 2–4. Amount in Controversy

As a means of limiting access to the federal courts, the Congress has included amount in controversy requirements in some of the jurisdictional statutes since the earliest days. Until 1980, when the requirement was eliminated entirely for federal question cases, actions brought under general federal question jurisdiction or diversity required that the matter in controversy exceed $10,000, exclusive of interest and costs. In 1988 the amount was raised to $50,000. Today, this prerequisite acts to assure that only the more significant diversity cases (in terms of size) reach the federal courts and in this way it controls the federal court caseload. Further, it protects small litigants from what may be the increased costs of federal court litigation.

Perhaps because amount in controversy requirements are merely judicial housekeeping measures and not constitutional barriers, the test for ascertaining whether they have been met is quite liberal. If the sum claimed by the plaintiff is made in good faith and it is not clear to a legal certainty that more than $50,000 will not be recovered, the requirement is met. In suits seeking injunctive relief, the amount in controversy typically is established by looking at the cost to the plaintiff if relief is denied, in other words the value of the right sought to be protected against defendant's interference. However, some courts have tested the requirement in terms of the amount it will cost the defendant to comply with the proposed injunction. The burden is placed on the defendant to show that the minimum amount is not involved. If it becomes apparent during the course of the trial or at the entry of the judgment that less than the requisite amount is involved, the case need not be dismissed for lack of subject-matter jurisdiction at that time. Rather, the statute provides that the court may assess costs against the plaintiff. 28 U.S.C.A. § 1332(b). In practice this measure is used infrequently and typically will be applied only when the plaintiff has acted in clear bad faith.

The largest difficulties in applying the amount in controversy requirement have arisen in cases involving multiple parties and multiple claims. The problem is how to value the amount in controversy when some of the claims are jurisdictionally sufficient and others are not, or when no individual claim involves the requisite amount, but the sum total of all the claims being asserted is more than $50,000. Most commonly, the issue is phrased in terms of whether aggregation is proper, although the question whether a claim seeking less than the minimum allowed can be heard when the court already has before it a jurisdictionally sufficient claim may be analyzed in terms of whether the court should exercise supplemental jurisdiction over the claim below the jurisdictional amount. See § 2–5, below.

The general rules governing aggregation of claims are the following. In a simple two-party action between A and B, A may join all the claims related and unrelated she has against B and aggregation will be allowed. When aggregation of only A's claims is involved there is at least the possibility that if they are all sustained, more than the jurisdictional minimum will be recovered. However, A will not be allowed to aggregate her claims with any counterclaims made by B in order to meet the applicable amount in the controversy requirement. To allow aggregation in that situation would permit the parties to consent to subject-matter jurisdiction indirectly and that is impermissible. Further, if both claims are valid, the claim and counterclaim will set-off one another and there will be no possibility that more than $50,000 will be recovered.

In multiple party litigation in which two plaintiffs (A & B) sue C or one plaintiff, A, sues two defendants (C & D) and in which no single claim meets the amount requisite, the courts generally have upheld jurisdiction only when both plaintiffs, A & B or both defendants, C & D, have a "joint and common interest" in the subject matter of the action, rather than "several interests" or interests that are "separate and distinct." This test also has been applied to class actions: each class member must possess a claim above the jurisdictional minimum, unless the members possess a joint and common interest in the action. Zahn v. International Paper Co. (S.Ct.1973); Snyder v. Harris (S.Ct. 1969).

What constitutes a joint and common interest has plagued the courts and commentators for years and is incapable of precise delineation. Suffice it to say that the requirement will be satisfied only in a small class of cases in which the law essentially has ruled that various interests are to be treated as one. For example, a husband and wife are deemed to hold a joint interest in their home in community property states. Partners similarly possess a joint interest in the partnership assets. However, the fact that the parties are united in interest in terms of desiring the same relief or resisting the same claims does not give them a joint and common interest. A parent seeking damages for injuries to his minor child and reimbursement for the medical expenses that were incurred on behalf of the child cannot aggregate those claims so as to be able to obtain federal court jurisdiction. The personal injury claim belongs to the child and the medical expenses claim represents damage to the parent; the parent-child relationship in itself does not create a joint and common interest in the action. Consequently, it is necessary to analyze the facts of each case carefully in light of past precedent to determine whether this requirement has been met.

§ 2–5. Supplemental Jurisdiction

In 1990, Congress enacted a statute authorizing what was termed "supplemental jurisdiction" over all related claims that are part of the same case or controversy as claims in the action that are within the court's original jurisdiction. 28 U.S.C.A. § 1367(a). The statute represents a codification of two forms of nonstatutory subject-matter jurisdiction developed earlier by the courts—ancillary and pendent jurisdiction. Thus, a brief look at those two forms of jurisdiction provides necessary background to understanding the current scope of supplemental jurisdiction.

Ancillary and pendent jurisdiction were developed by the courts for use in multiple claim actions in order to permit entire disputes to be tried in the federal courts, thereby avoiding multiple actions. Both types of jurisdiction required the presence in the suit of at least one claim that met the standards of one of the statutory bases for subject-matter jurisdiction. Jurisdiction then could be allowed over some otherwise jurisdictionally insufficient claim if that claim arose out of the same core of aggregate fact or, stated alternatively, if both claims arose out of a common nucleus of operative fact, or the same transaction or occurrence. Given the liberal claim and party joinder provisions in the federal rules, see §§ 3–11—3–20, below, these bases for jurisdiction frequently were invoked.

Although the test governing the assertion of both ancillary and pendent jurisdiction was basically the same, the terms technically applied to different types of situations. Historically, pendent jurisdiction was invoked when the question presented was whether a state law claim could be asserted by a party who already was presenting a federal question claim. Ancillary jurisdiction pertained to all other situations in which the federal court retained jurisdiction over closely related claims that were jurisdictionally insufficient by themselves, but were attached to jurisdictionally proper claims.

The assertion of this jurisdictional power was deemed constitutional under Article III, section 2 because the courts merely were defining what constituted "a case or controversy" in a multiple claim situation. The rationale supporting the extension of federal court jurisdiction to ancillary and pendent claims was primarily one of judicial economy—to rule otherwise would require the plaintiff to file two suits, one in federal and the other in state court. Further, the availability of pendent jurisdiction made the federal court a viable alternative to the state courts in which all the claims could be joined.

The leading Supreme Court case setting out the standard for assessing whether ancillary or pendent jurisdiction could be asserted was United Mine Workers of America v. Gibbs (S.Ct.1966). The Court set forth a two-part analysis, which remains controlling today.

The first question that must be asked is whether the claim meets the standard for asserting this type of jurisdiction—is there a common nucleus of operative fact between the jurisdictionally sufficient and insufficient claims? Illustratively, an action asserting a federal antitrust claim and a state unfair competition claim usually will meet this standard. Many of the facts that must be proven to show unfair competition also will aid in demonstrating price-fixing or a monopoly, which would violate the federal law. On the other hand, a slander claim will require proof of different facts than a personal injury claim. This is true even if the defendant allegedly slandered the plaintiff immediately after running into her with his automobile so that the events giving rise to the claims were part of a series.

Once the court determines that it has the power to decide the entire case, it then must decide the second question: whether taking the otherwise jurisdictionally insufficient claim will foster judicial economy and will be fair to the parties. Thus, the actual assertion of ancillary or pendent jurisdiction was discretionary. A wide range of factors could be taken into account in deciding this discretionary issue and the court could review the exercise of its discretion throughout the case. For example, if the claims that independently met subject-matter jurisdiction requirements were dismissed at an early stage in a lawsuit, judicial economy may suggest that the ancillary or pendent claims also should be dismissed and the parties left to litigate those issues in the state courts. Similarly, if the state issues presented by a proposed ancillary or pendent claim were peculiarly difficult or novel, jurisdiction might be declined in order to allow the state courts to rule on those questions. If the presence of the additional claims or parties would produce jury confusion that could not be controlled in other ways, jurisdiction also might be refused. In any case in which pendent or ancillary jurisdiction was not allowed, only the additional claims were dismissed, the federal court continued to decide the jurisdictionally proper claims before it.

The expansion of pendent and ancillary jurisdiction to embrace situations in which additional parties as well as claims are involved presented serious difficulties for the courts. Ancillary jurisdiction traditionally included the introduction of claims by intervenors of right (see § 3–18, below), as well as the bringing in of third-party defendants by defendants (see § 3–16, below). Several lower federal courts thus also expanded pendent jurisdiction notions to include situations involving party joinder, developing what was referred to as pendent-party jurisdiction. Under this approach, a plaintiff could sue two defendants, asserting a jurisdictionally sufficient claim against one and a related but insufficient claim against the other. A similar result could occur when two or more plaintiffs joined in a suit against a single defendant.

The validity of pendent-party jurisdiction first was called into question by the Supreme Court in Aldinger v. Howard (S.Ct.1976). There the Court stated that in addition to finding that the claims arose out of a common transaction, it was necessary to consider whether there was anything in the statute conferring jurisdiction over the proper claim suggesting that the Congress would not approve the extension of jurisdiction over the additional party. Using this standard, the Court in a later case struck down an attempt to use ancillary jurisdiction concepts to authorize a plaintiff in a diversity case to assert a claim against a nondiverse third-party defendant, finding that attempt violative of the diversity statute's requirement of complete diversity. Owen Equipment & Erection Co. v. Kroger (S.Ct. 1978). The Court distinguished other cases allowing ancillary jurisdiction to be used to assert counterclaims, cross-claims and impleader claims on the ground that in those suits the additional claims were logically dependent on the main claim and were being asserted by defendants who had not chosen the forum in which to sue. In 1989, the Supreme Court in Finley v. United States (S.Ct. 1989), suggested an even much narrower view of pendent-party jurisdiction, holding that although the extension of pendent-party jurisdiction might be constitutional, in the absence of statutory authorization for it, the courts were powerless to create it. In response, the Congress enacted the 1990 supplemental jurisdiction statute.

The availability of supplemental jurisdiction is governed by the Gibbs standard of whether the insufficient claims share a common nucleus of operative fact with the sufficient claims so as to constitute the same case or controversy. This jurisdiction may be invoked even if additional parties are joined, as long as the basis for jurisdiction over the main claims is not solely diversity. 28 U.S.C.A. § 1367(b). Like traditional pendent jurisdiction, the exercise of jurisdiction under this new statute is discretionary and the court may decline to exercise it in deference to state interests. 28 U.S.C.A. § 1367(c). Thus, prior case law interpreting and applying Gibbs remains pertinent under the statute.

In its treatment of diversity actions the statute has introduced some important jurisdictional changes, as well as ambiguities. See 28 U.S.C.A. § 1367(b). First, intervenors no longer are deemed ancillary, even though their claims are intimately bound up with the main action. If their claims or the claims by the plaintiff against them do not independently satisfy the diversity statute, they cannot intervene because supplemental jurisdiction is prohibited. Second, it now appears under the language of the statute that although a nondiverse third-party defendant can invoke supplemental jurisdiction to assert a claim directly against the plaintiff, the plaintiff cannot invoke the statute to assert a counterclaim in response. Finally, because the statute is silent regarding the amount in controversy requirement, some lower federal courts have allowed it to be invoked to uphold jurisdiction over claims not meeting the jurisdictional minimum. Other courts have disagreed, finding that that result would be contrary to prior law (see § 2–4, above) and that there was no congressional intent to overrule that law.

§ 2–6. Removal Jurisdiction

When concurrent jurisdiction is placed in the federal and state courts, the plaintiff may choose in which one to file suit. If plaintiff opts for state court, the defendant may be able to get the suit to the federal court in that district if the defendant can show that the case falls within the special federal statute designed for that purpose, 28 U.S.C.A. § 1441. In a two-party single claim action there are three prerequisites to removal. First, removal is proper only if the federal court would have had jurisdiction had the plaintiff opted to begin the action there. 28 U.S.C.A. § 1441(a). The fact that venue would have been improper in the federal court will not preclude removal. Only jurisdictional defects will act as a bar. In light of the well-pleaded complaint rule, see § 2–2, above, this means that removal cannot be based on a federal question in the defendant's answer or on the fact that a federal counterclaim is being asserted. The plaintiff's complaint must present a basis for federal court jurisdiction. Removal jurisdiction in multiclaim or multiple party actions thus may be proper if the plaintiff could have utilized supplemental jurisdiction (see § 2–5, above) for the state law claims for which there is no independent basis of jurisdiction. Second, only defendants can remove. 28 U.S.C.A. § 1441(a). Plaintiffs cannot remove even if the defendant interposes a counterclaim so that they are then "defending parties." Shamrock Oil & Gas Corp. v. Sheets (S.Ct.1941). Third, in cases based on diversity of citizenship only nonresident defendants can remove. 28 U.S.C.A. § 1441(b).

The removal statute also contains special authorization for removal in certain federal question cases involving multiple parties or claims that otherwise would not be removable. 28 U.S.C.A. § 1441(c). The purpose of this provision is to prevent the plaintiff from blocking the defendant's option simply by including some nonremovable claims or parties and to make the defendant's choice of the federal court a viable one. Removal is permissible if the defendant can show that a claim exists that could have been brought in federal court under general federal question jurisdiction and that that claim is "separate and independent" from the other nonremovable claims. However, once the action is removed, the federal court may exercise its discretion to remand to the state court "matters in which State law predominates." Thus, if state matters inhere in the federal law claim as well as the separate state law claims, the court may exercise its discretion to remand the entire case to the state courts under this provision. This is in contrast to the court's discretionary decision under supplemental jurisdiction, which is limited to dismissing only the jurisdictionally insufficient claim. See § 2–5, above.

Removal jurisdiction raises serious federalism concerns as it presents a situation in which the federal court is taking a case away from a state court, albeit at the request of a party. This fact is emphasized by the removal procedure itself. The defendant in the state court action files the removal petition in the federal court. See 28 U.S.C.A. § 1446(a). A copy of the petition is filed simultaneously in the state court and written notice is given to the other parties. As stated in the federal removal statute, "the State court shall proceed no further unless and until the case is remanded." 28 U.S.C.A. § 1446(d). A plaintiff who wishes to challenge removal must do so by filing a motion to remand in the federal court. The desire to afford the defendant the opportunity to invoke federal jurisdiction is deemed to outweigh concerns about the potential impact of removal on federal-state court relations. Nonetheless, a federal court deciding whether to remand some state claims that are before it only because of the operation of Section 1441 may be influenced by federalism notions to return to the state court those claims not clearly or inextricably entwined with the claims meeting ordinary federal jurisdiction standards.

B.　VENUE

§ 2–7.　General Principles Governing

Venue is a statutory requirement designed to regulate the flow of judicial business within a particular court system and to identify a convenient forum for the parties to litigate their dispute. In the federal court system, venue provisions set out the district or districts in a given state in which suit may be brought, assuming subject-matter and personal jurisdiction requirements are met.   In state court systems, venue statutes typically refer to the proper county in which to bring the action.   Once it has been determined whether an action can be filed in state or federal court, §§ 2–1—2–4, above, and in which states personal jurisdiction may be obtained over the defendant, §§ 2–10—2–20, below, the applicable venue statutes must be consulted in order to further identify which courts within those judicial systems are permissible fora.

Although the types of venue statutes vary, some discussion of their characteristics may be helpful. A common provision that is utilized places venue for transitory causes of action at the residence of the defendant.   See Cal.Civ.Proc.Code § 395(a). The residence of a corporation has been established statutorily in some states as the corporation's principal place of business.   See Cal.Civ.Proc.Code § 395.5.   As a result of a 1988 amendment to the general federal venue statute, the standard for finding venue in federal court actions against corporations has been identified with the test for asserting jurisdiction over them.   Corporate defendants are deemed to reside in any district in which they are subject to personal jurisdiction at the time the action commences.   See 28 U.S.C.A. § 1391(c). More specific venue provisions may be tied to the kind of action being brought (e.g. tort, contract) and may identify the locale of specific events (e.g. the performance of the contract, tortious injury) as a convenient place to bring suit. In the federal system, the general venue statute, which was amended in 1992, now provides that in actions based on diversity of citizenship, venue is proper in any district where a defendant resides, in a district where "a substantial part of the events or omissions giving rise to the claim occurred, or a substantial part of property that is the subject of the action is situated," or, in cases with multiple defendants, in a district where any of the defendants are subject to personal jurisdiction when the suit is commenced, if there is no other district where the action can be brought. 28 U.S.C.A. § 1391(a). In federal question actions, this last provision is broadened to provide that venue may be laid in any district where any defendant may be found, if there is no other district where the action otherwise can be brought. 28 U.S.C.A. § 1391(b)(3). In cases in which more than one venue may be proper, the plaintiff can choose where to file suit.

The propriety of the venue is determined at the outset of the action. If additional claims are filed, such as third-party claims or intervention claims, the venue requirements typically will not be applied to those claims. Courts commonly invoke notions of waiver or ancillary venue in these circumstances. When a counterclaim is asserted against the plaintiff, it is said that by filing suit plaintiff consented to the convenience of the forum. These approaches to venue over additional claims rest on the sound premise that if the forum is established as a convenient one at the outset of the litigation, it will remain so for the parties and all their claims. Thus, unlike subject-matter and personal jurisdiction, venue need not be tested each time a claim is added to the action.

Notably, the fact that the forum chosen meets statutory venue requirements does not guarantee that it necessarily will be the most convenient one for a particular dispute. Thus, as is discussed later, even though an action is filed in compliance with the venue statute, it later may be dismissed or transferred to a more convenient locale. See § 2–30, below.

§ 2–8. Local Action Principle

A common distinction that is drawn in venue statutes is the difference between a local and a transitory action. Local actions are those which involve ownership of, possession of, or injury to real property. Transitory actions encompass all other suits. Historically, because of the desire to have juries who were familiar with the facts of the case, local actions could be brought only in the county in which the land was situated. Transitory actions were not so restricted.

The local action principle may be viewed as a venue rule, regulating the business of the courts within a state. When applied across state lines its significance increases because it becomes entwined with notions of state sovereignty over real property within a given state's borders. Based on the local action principle, the United States Supreme Court held that a court in the county or district in which land is situated may refuse to give full faith and credit to a judgment or decree of another state's court which affects the title to that land, even though the parties were within the personal jurisdiction of the forum court at the time the judgment was entered. Fall v. Eastin (S.Ct.1909). This seems to elevate the local action principle to one of constitutional magnitude, an anomalous result in our federal system. Whether it is appropriate to consider the local action principle as grounded in jurisdictional concerns or merely as a specialized venue restraint is predominantly a matter of academic interest. All modern state decisions have ruled that full faith and credit will be given, even though it is not required, and thus the principle has not produced significant problems in modern times.

C. PERSONAL JURISDICTION

§ 2–9. Introduction

The doctrine of personal jurisdiction addresses the question whether a court has the power to render a binding, enforceable judgment defining or declaring the rights and duties of the parties. As to plaintiffs, the very act of seeking relief always has been supposed to constitute a submission to jurisdiction, warranting a judgment against them. When the proposed defendant resides in and is present in the state in which the court is sitting, the question has posed few problems; power is assumed to exist because each state has sovereign control over all things and persons within its borders. In those cases the question becomes whether jurisdiction has been obtained in compliance with proper procedural requirements and with adequate notification.

Historically, the only real difficulty in applying these territorial principles involved corporations, because corporations are only legal constructs and have no tangible existence and thus no visible situs. This problem first was solved by holding that a corporation always was subject to the jurisdiction of the courts under whose laws it was incorporated. The courts later added to this notion the rule that a corporation also was subject to suit when it had "consented" expressly or impliedly to be sued in a particular state. See § 2–15, below. This consent theory quickly verged on the fictitious so courts added another concept seeking to equate corporations and natural persons. Because the physical presence of a person was deemed enough, a corporation was declared "present" and thus within a particular state's personal jurisdiction reach when the extent and continuity of its business activities in the state seemed large enough to equate activity with presence. Under this "presence" approach, the discontinuance of corporate activities, like the departure of an individual, terminated the state's power to enter a binding, enforceable judgment. This limitation on the court's power was true even though the defendant was being sued on the basis of its earlier activities in the state.

Thus, perhaps not surprisingly, the major jurisdictional problems and developments have centered on the issue whether and when a court can assert personal jurisdiction over a defendant not found within the state. To answer this question usually requires two steps. First, you must find a statute authorizing the assertion of personal jurisdiction over persons outside the forum state's borders under circumstances similar to your case. See §§ 2–10—2–12, below. Second, you must be able to conclude that the application of the statute to the case at hand meets constitutional standards. See §§ 2–16—2–20, below. Both these steps must be satisfied for each and every defendant in an action, as well as any additional parties who later may be joined.

The development of state statutes and of the constitutional standard applied to extraterritorial assertions of personal jurisdiction has undergone several twists and turns. In particular, in a series of decisions beginning in 1977, the Supreme Court added some important refinements to the constitutional standard applicable to all assertions of personal jurisdiction. Thus, a complete study of this area of procedure requires an analysis of Supreme Court decisions, a close look at a number of the statutes that have been adopted, and a review of lower court decisions that have applied and interpreted these developments. After an abbreviated review of the historic premises from which the modern law of personal jurisdiction developed, the primary focus in this Nutshell will be on modern jurisdictional theory.

Finally, in addition to fitting your case within a statute and making certain that the use of that statute is consistent with the Constitution, procedural due process concerns also require that persons whose rights will be affected by any judgment be given adequate notice and an opportunity to be heard. See § 2–21 and § 6–4, below. This means that the method used to assert jurisdiction must be designed to comport with those requirements. Otherwise, any judgment that is entered may be invalid.

Necessarily, the discussion in this Nutshell of each of these elements of obtaining proper personal jurisdiction must be somewhat brief. Readers who would like a more complete treatment of these matters should refer to J. Friedenthal, M. Kane & A. Miller, *Civil Procedure* Ch. 3 (2d ed.1993).

1. STATUTORY SOURCES OF JURISDICTIONAL POWER

a. State Courts

§ 2–10. Types of Statutes

There are two types of statutes that may be consulted to determine whether a state may assert jurisdiction over a nonresident defendant who is outside the borders of the state. The first type (commonly called a long-arm statute) specifically authorizes the state courts to exert extraterritorial jurisdiction over defendants who meet the conditions set out in the statute. Alternatively, if the defendant owns property in the state, then it may be possible to assert jurisdiction based on the attachment of that property at the outset of the suit. In that situation, it is necessary to determine whether the state has an attachment statute, authorizing the seizure of the defendant's property. If no long-arm or attachment statute covering the case at hand exists, personal jurisdiction cannot be asserted over the out-of-state defendant.

Although state long-arm statutes are many and varied, a brief description may be helpful. The primary differentiating characteristic between long-arm statutes is the amount of detailed requirements or categories that are set out. At one end of the spectrum are those statutes permitting the assertion of jurisdiction whenever the defendant has the necessary minimum contacts with the state and jurisdiction would not be contrary to the constitution or laws of the United States. See, e.g., R.I.Gen.L. § 9–5–33, Cal.Civ.Proc.Code § 410.10. These vague statutory standards allow the courts to stretch their jurisdiction to its furthest possible limits. They also are easy to apply in an era of increasing travel and changing business arrangements because the statute can be invoked for new and different situations without any need to fit the case into a definition or category that was included for other purposes. However, this fluidity has drawbacks. Every jurisdiction question becomes a constitutional one and the prognosis for when jurisdiction will be upheld is more difficult to make because of the vagueness of the standard.

At the other end of the spectrum, some statutes list in great detail the kinds of activities on the part of nonresidents for which extraterritorial jurisdiction may be asserted. For example, all fifty states had nonresident motorist statutes, providing for the assertion of jurisdiction over nonresidents who have driven into the state and caused an accident there. Other common acts for which long-arm jurisdiction may be asserted are: the transaction of business in the state, contracting to supply goods or services in the state, the commission of a tortious act in the state, the commission of a tortious act outside the state that causes injury in the state, coupled with some other business activity of defendant in the state, and the ownership, use or possession of real property in a state. See, e.g., N.Y.C.P.L.R. 302(a); Uniform Interstate & Int'l Pro.Act § 1.03. Other states have focused on the kind of action being brought (e.g. contract, tort) and have set out the conduct on the part of the defendant that will justify the assertion of long-arm jurisdiction in those types of suits. See, e.g., N.C.Gen.Stat. § 1–75–4. If an action does not fit into any of the categories listed in these more specific statutes, long-arm jurisdiction cannot be asserted.

State attachment statutes vary in the procedural requirements that are necessary to effectuate a proper attachment. Further, those requirements must meet the constitutional standards developed by the Supreme Court to ensure adequate notice and an opportunity to be heard. See § 6–4, below. Most states also have limited the availability of their attachment statutes to certain prescribed situations, such as when the defendant, with the intent to defraud creditors, has assigned, secreted, disposed of or removed property from the state, or is about to do so. See, e.g., N.Y.—McKinney's CPLR 6201. Thus, it is important to consult local law carefully in order to determine whether and how jurisdiction may be asserted by attachment.

b.   Federal Courts

§ 2–11.   General Rules Governing

Although the Congress could enact legislation governing the assertion of personal jurisdiction by the federal courts, with few exceptions, see § 2–12, below, it has not done so. The courts are limited in their exercise of long-arm jurisdiction to the situations set out in Rule 4 and cannot simply extend their jurisdiction as a matter of federal common law. Omni Capital Int'l v. Rudolf Wolff & Co. (S.Ct.1987).

Federal Rule 4(k) sets out the territorial limits of federal court service of process. In the absence of federal legislation specifically authorizing long-arm jurisdiction, a federal court may exercise jurisdiction over a defendant outside the boundaries of the state in which it is sitting in one of three circumstances.

First, the court can refer to the statutes and rules governing out-of-state service that exist in the state in which it is sitting. Federal courts may utilize state long-arm statutes or any state statute allowing the attachment of property owned by nonresidents in order to obtain jurisdiction over a nonresident defendant. Thus, the ability of a federal court to enter a binding, enforceable judgment against an out-of-state defendant often is the same as the state courts of the state in which it is sitting.

Second, Federal Rule 4(k)(1)(B) authorizes service of process within one hundred miles of the federal courthouse for certain additional parties to the action. In many instances this 100–mile bulge provision will not act extraterritorially as the court may be so situated that a one hundred mile radius is still within the state. However, in other cases the application of the provision will result in long-arm jurisdiction being obtained, despite the absence of any applicable state long-arm statute.

The third situation when a federal court may be able to exert jurisdiction over parties outside the state in which it sits was added to Rule 4 in 1993. It pertains if the underlying claims in the action arise under federal law and the defendant is not otherwise subject to the general jurisdiction of any state. Fed.Rule 4(k)(2). This would occur, for example, if the defendant is from a foreign country and his conduct was not such that it fit within the scope of any existing state long-arm provisions.

§ 2–12. Specialized Provisions

The few federal long-arm provisions that exist are part of statutes establishing particular federal causes of action. For example, in actions brought under the antitrust or the federal securities laws there are no geographic boundaries to the federal courts jurisdiction. 15 U.S.C.A. §§ 4 and 78aa. Similarly, in federal interpleader actions in which a stakeholder with a limited fund to which there are conflicting claims is seeking a ruling as to how the fund should be distributed, a federal statute authorizes nationwide service of process, eliminating any limitations on the federal courts personal jurisdiction. 28 U.S.C.A. § 2361. (See § 8–7, below.) Although these provisions are few in number, it is wise in actions based on federal law to check the statute on which your claim is based to determine if a special long-arm provision is available.

2.　STANDARD FOR ASSERTING PERSONAL JURISDICTION

a.　Traditional Bases

§ 2–13.　Sovereignty: The Territoriality Theory

Personal jurisdiction doctrine originally rested on notions of sovereignty. Since each state had exclusive power over all persons within its borders, it could render binding judgments in any suits brought against those persons. This jurisdiction typically was referred to as *in personam*. In personam jurisdiction was premised on the presence of the individual defendant in the state at the time the action was commenced. It mattered not whether the defendant's presence was temporary, as in the case of a transient, or more permanent. On the other hand, in personam jurisdiction was not al-

lowed over persons outside the state borders because that would violate another state's sovereignty. A valid in personam judgment was entitled to
full faith and credit in all the sister states under
Article IV, Section 1 of the United States Constitution.

The state also had sovereign power over all property within its borders and it was held that a state
court could render a valid and enforceable judgment
concerning the ownership of or title to in-state
property, regardless of the whereabouts of the defendant. This form of personal jurisdiction was
termed *in rem*. Because of the state's exclusive
control over the property, any judgment entered in
such an action would "bind the world" and other
states would be required to give it full faith and
credit.

Notions of sovereignty were not as limited as the
preceding description might suggest. For example,
in personam jurisdiction based on the defendant's
domicile and even a defendant's national citizenship
was upheld. Milliken v. Meyer (S.Ct.1940); Blackmer v. United States (S.Ct.1932). It was reasoned
that the sovereign could command certain obligations and duties from its citizens even when they
were not physically present in the jurisdiction.
Similarly, in cases involving the marital status of a
resident plaintiff and a defendant who no longer
was a resident, jurisdiction was upheld based on the
notion that the state had sovereign power over the
legal status of its domiciliaries and necessarily must
be able to render a binding decree on the status of

its resident plaintiff. Finally, nonresidents who owned property within a state were deemed within the state's in personam jurisdiction on causes of action arising out of that property. A nonresident landlord could be sued for injuries caused by the failure to maintain the property in a safe condition. The state's sovereign control over the property allowed it to enter an enforceable judgment against any landlord who wants the privilege of owning property in the state.

The most important expansion in the law of sovereignty as applied to personal jurisdiction came with the development of *quasi in rem* jurisdiction. In quasi in rem jurisdiction cases, property within a state was used as a vehicle to reach the defendant in order to adjudicate personal rights that might or might not be related to the property. Thus, a plaintiff might invoke quasi in rem jurisdiction in order to secure a preexisting claim to the property, such as in a suit for specific performance of a contract to convey land. When used this way, quasi in rem jurisdiction differed from in rem jurisdiction primarily because the property was important only to the remedy, it did not involve the underlying substantive right to relief, which was premised on contract law. Alternatively, quasi in rem jurisdiction could be used when the personal rights at issue were totally unrelated to the property. When used this way, this form of jurisdiction was sometimes referred to as attachment jurisdiction.

When asserting either form of quasi in rem jurisdiction, the state asserted its sovereign power by attaching or seizing the property at the commencement of the action. Then, utilizing the fiction that the property was a manifestation of the defendant, the court adjudicated the personal claim before it. A defendant who entered to defend, submitted himself to the in personam jurisdiction of the court and a binding judgment for the full amount claimed could be entered in the event that the plaintiff prevailed on the merits. If the defendant did not appear and defaulted, the judgment was limited to the value of the property attached because, in keeping with the fiction, that was the limit of the state's sovereign power. No full faith and credit would be given to the judgment beyond that amount. The plaintiff had to begin an entirely new action in order to obtain further relief.

Attachment of the property at the commencement was crucial to this form of jurisdiction. It substantiated the state's claim of power and, by preventing the property from being moved or sold during the action, it ensured the enforceability of any judgment the plaintiff might obtain. Pennoyer v. Neff (S.Ct.1877). Finally, attachment also served as a means of notifying the defendant of the proceedings.

Although the doctrine of quasi in rem jurisdiction originated in cases involving real property, where the state's sovereignty was deeply rooted in history, it gradually was expanded to apply to movable property, intangibles, and even contingent obligations. As is discussed in the following section, these latter developments caused a great degree of controversy.

§ 2-14. Intangibles and Contingent Obligations

The assertion of quasi in rem jurisdiction based on the presence of intangibles and contingent obligations in the forum state raised the problem of how to identify their situs. For example, bank deposits were deemed to be located at the bank with which the defendant did business and stock commonly was deemed to be present wherever the stock certificates were located. One of the most controversial applications of quasi in rem jurisdiction was the ruling by the United States Supreme Court in Harris v. Balk (S.Ct.1904). The Court held that a debt resides with the debtor. By locating the debt with the debtor, a creditor (A) could obtain attachment jurisdiction over a nonresident debtor (B) if B were owed money by another person (C) and C came into A's state and was served with process there. If C contested the fact that a debt was owed to B, then A could not obtain quasi in rem jurisdiction over B. In personam jurisdiction over B would be needed in order to be able to enter a judgment declaring that the debt between B and C existed. New York Life Ins. Co. v. Dunlevy (S.Ct.1916). Until that question was decided, there was no property within the state on which the court could base quasi in rem jurisdiction. If C conceded the obligation, then in-state service of process on C permitted the court to invoke the fiction that the debt as property of B was within its sovereign reach and thus, it could render a judgment on the unrelated claim of A against B that was enforceable against

that property. Under this reasoning, B was subject
to attachment jurisdiction wherever his peripatetic
debtor might wander. The nonresident debtor was
afforded some protection in this scheme by the fact
that the seized debtor had to notify him of the
proceedings in order to escape being forced to pay
again. However, notice did not affect the original
court's jurisdiction, it merely protected C from double liability.

An even more controversial application of quasi
in rem jurisdiction was developed in New York
where the courts applied the analysis just described
to allow jurisdiction based on an insurer's contingent obligation to defend and indemnify its insured.
Seider v. Roth (N.Y.1966). The approach taken was
as follows. A, a New York resident, was injured in
an automobile accident in some other state by B, a
nonresident of New York. B was insured by I, a
large corporation doing business in New York, as
well as in other states. A sued B in New York by
attaching I's duty to defend and indemnify. Quasi
in rem jurisdiction was allowed because of the
state's sovereign power over I. The controversy
over this form of attachment lies in the contingent
nature of the debt: if the insured is found to be free
from negligence, then there is no debt; the debt
exists only if the plaintiff wins. Thus, jurisdiction
is extended on the basis of something that does not
yet, and may never, exist. Again, some protection
was afforded to ameliorate the apparent harshness
of this doctrine by allowing the defendant to make a
limited appearance and defend on the merits with-

out consenting to in personam jurisdiction. (See § 2–28, below.) The judgment remained limited to the face amount of the policy. Further, the New York courts ruled that the plaintiff had to be a resident or the cause of action had to arise in New York before jurisdiction could be asserted.

The two developments just described represent the furthest extensions by the courts of sovereignty as a basis for personal jurisdiction. Perhaps not surprisingly, a majority of states refused to follow the lead of New York in the insurance field, and other courts and commentators suggested that the fairness of asserting jurisdiction under these circumstances was of prime importance. In an era that emphasizes fairness as the lynchpin for the assertion of jurisdiction (see § 2–16, below), theories resting solely on sheer power and fictions regarding the situs of intangibles were an anomaly.

§ 2–15. Consent

A party always may concede a court's authority to render a binding, enforceable judgment against him. In some cases consent may be explicit, as when it is in a contract. In others notions of waiver act as implied consent. This may occur by the failure of the defendant to comply with the applicable rules governing the methods of raising jurisdictional objections, see § 2–27, below. In the case of a nonresident plaintiff faced with counterclaims in her own action, the entry into the forum to institute the action will be deemed submission to the state's jurisdiction.

Historically, finding that a nonresident defendant had impliedly consented to jurisdiction prior to the filing of a lawsuit served as a prime basis for asserting in personam jurisdiction over a mobile, business citizenry when a strict application of sovereignty principles would not permit jurisdiction. In the corporate field it was held that a state could exclude a nonresident corporation from doing business in the state. Thus, some states enacted legislation requiring out-of-state businesses to consent to jurisdiction as a condition of doing business in the state by appointing an agent in the state to receive process for them. Other states designated a state official in their statutes as the agent for receipt of process for nonresident corporations and provided that all corporations doing business thereafter impliedly consented to suit in the state in actions arising out of their activities there. The fact that the corporation no longer was doing business in the state at the time an action was commenced did not affect the court's jurisdiction because of the corporation's prior implied consent to suit.

But the consent theory had its limitations. For example, when implied consent was used, jurisdiction could be asserted only for causes of action arising out of the business done in the forum state. Jurisdiction based on express consent was not so limited. However, in that situation, the termination of corporate activities within the state acted as a negation of consent and jurisdiction no longer could be asserted even in suits directly arising out of forum state activities of the corporation before it left the state.

In cases involving individuals, implied consent became an important justification for the assertion of jurisdiction over nonresident motorists who were alleged to have harmed resident plaintiffs. Utilizing their state police power (a direct manifestation of state sovereignty), states enacted nonresident motorist or single-act statutes, authorizing their courts to assert in personam jurisdiction over nonresident defendants when their sole contact with the state was the accident giving rise to the action and a resident plaintiff was injured. The fiction utilized was that the defendant had impliedly consented to jurisdiction by driving on the highways once the long-arm statute had been enacted. Hess v. Pawloski (S.Ct.1927). Later decisions expanded the application of these statutes to cases involving nonresident plaintiffs. Despite the movement away from utilizing fictions as the basis for asserting jurisdiction, these statutes remain valid today because the limited type of jurisdiction they authorize should be permissible even under more modern jurisdictional theories. See § 2-20, below.

b.　Modern Standards

§ 2-16.　The In Personam Wing: Minimum Contacts, "Fair Play and Substantial Justice"

With the increasing movement of individuals between states and the expansion of corporate activities on a national scale, the limitations of the sovereignty and consent theories became apparent. Although the courts continued to rely on expanding sovereignty notions as the means of supporting in rem and quasi in rem jurisdiction, increased emphasis was placed on more general due process principles as providing the major limitation on a court's power to assert in personam jurisdiction over a nonresident outside its state's borders.

The Supreme Court clearly enunciated the principles underlying this due process approach to in personam jurisdiction in International Shoe Co. v. Washington (S.Ct.1945). The test enunciated by the Court was that the defendant should have sufficient "minimum contacts" with the forum state so that traditional notions of "fair play and substantial justice" would not be offended by the assertion of jurisdiction there.

International Shoe presents a two-pronged test. First, minimum contacts must be shown and second, the court must find that the forum is a fair one in which the defendant will have a full opportunity to be heard. While these two determinations necessarily overlap, they have independent significance and meeting one will not justify ignoring the other. For example, the fact that the forum state is convenient because many of the witnesses and parties are there, does not in itself warrant the assertion of jurisdiction. The court still must find that the defendant has the requisite minimum contacts with the state to support jurisdiction. Indeed, the importance of the minimum contacts portion of the

Shoe standard was underscored in World–Wide Volkswagen Corp. v. Woodson (S.Ct.1980), when the Supreme Court characterized the minimum contacts inquiry as a threshold question. The failure to cross that threshold meant that various facts suggesting that the particular forum chosen was fair or convenient were irrelevant.

Additional content has been given to the meaning of "minimum contacts" by numerous Supreme Court decisions since International Shoe. The Court has noted repeatedly that the defendant's contact with the forum must be purposeful—the court must be able to find that the defendant has purposefully availed himself of the privilege of conducting some activity in the state, thereby invoking the benefits and protections of state law. Hanson v. Denckla (S.Ct.1958). The need to show purposeful conduct has proved a significant barrier to the assertion of jurisdiction in numerous cases. For example, a divorced father who cooperated with his children's desire to go to live with their mother was not subject to jurisdiction in the mother's state in a suit for child custody and increased child support. The sending of the children to the mother was not deemed a purposeful act, it was mere acquiescence in their request. Further, the father derived no economic benefit from the forum state as a result of the change. Kulko v. Superior Court (S.Ct.1978). And in an Oklahoma case arising out of a car accident in the forum state, the Supreme Court ruled that jurisdiction could not be asserted over the New York auto retailer and the regional distributor because neither of those defendants had purposefully attempted to serve the Oklahoma market. It was not sufficient that they might derive revenue and benefit from the fact that the cars they marketed were mobile and thus could be used in Oklahoma. The unilateral activity of the plaintiff car owners in driving to Oklahoma could not be used to suggest a benefit that would sustain jurisdiction—it was the defendant's conduct that was crucial. World–Wide Volkswagen Corp. v. Woodson (S.Ct. 1980).

On the other hand, although purposeful contact with the forum state is found most easily if the defendant actively conducts business in the state, deliberate activity outside the state that is aimed at obtaining some benefit, albeit indirect, from the forum state may satisfy this part of the Shoe standard. It is not clear whether it is sufficient that the defendant merely have purposefully entered its product into the general stream of commerce or whether it knowingly must have placed its product in a stream of commerce that was directed at the forum state. The Supreme Court in the Volkswagen case suggested that jurisdiction in Oklahoma could be asserted over the international manufacturer and the national importer of the allegedly defective auto because both of those entities purposefully entered the national market and received economic benefits from that market. However, in a later case, Asahi Metal Industry Co. v. Superior Court (S.Ct.1987), the Court was evenly divided on the question whether it was necessary to show that the defendant had to purposefully direct its product toward the forum state (California) or just the national market in order to constitute sufficient conduct to cross the minimum contacts threshold.

Under either view, the rationale for finding sufficient contact is that the defendant's conduct outside the state is of such a character that the defendant should reasonably foresee that if its product malfunctions in any state in the general market, it may be subject to suit where the problem occurred. Thus, the conduct of the defendant outside the state must be examined carefully to determine if it was of such a character that defendant should have foreseen having to defend in the forum state.

The quality and purposefulness of the defendant's contact with the state is related not only to foreseeability, but also to the notion that the defendant has obtained some benefit or privilege from the forum state so that it is fair to require the defendant to defend suit there. For example, in a products liability setting such as the Volkswagen case, the local retailer, in contrast to the manufacturer, has no way to foresee where an auto it sells may be driven. Further, it has done nothing itself to try to benefit economically from business with other states' citizens. Consequently, it cannot be held accountable in distant fora where the product later malfunctions. Similarly, the Supreme Court has noted that purchases and related trips into the forum state are not sufficient, standing alone, to sustain jurisdiction over a nonresident corporation for a claim unrelated to those purchase transactions. Helicopteros Nacionales de Colombia, S.A. v. Hall (S.Ct.1984).

Although reference to the defendant's foreseeability in being sued in the forum state may seem to inject a complex subjective inquiry into the minimum contacts standard, this is not necessarily so. First, as just noted, foreseeability may be satisfied easily if it is coupled with purposeful conduct outside the forum designed to somehow derive benefits from the forum state. Illustratively, when an intentional tort is involved, foreseeability should be easy to satisfy. Calder v. Jones (S.Ct.1984). And when an out-of-state party deliberately seeks and negotiates a long-term contract, envisioning continuing contacts with the forum, then it cannot claim that it is not foreseeable that it would have to defend a suit there involving a dispute arising out of that contract. Burger King Corp. v. Rudzewicz (S.Ct.1985).

Finally, it must be remembered that even if a defendant is shown to have crossed the minimum contacts threshold, jurisdiction still may not be upheld unless the court is able to find that its assertion is consistent with notions of fair play and substantial justice. No one factor is determinative. Keeton v. Hustler Magazine, Inc. (S.Ct.1984)(fact that plaintiff is a nonresident and chose the forum because of uniquely long statute of limitations is not determinative). Rather, the court will consider a number of factors, including the forum state's interest in regulating the activity involved or in providing a forum for its residents; the relative convenience to the parties of the tribunal chosen in terms of the witnesses, evidence and general location, as well as whether an alternative forum exists; the desire to avoid a multiplicity of lawsuits; and any other factor bearing on the fairness of the chosen forum. All of the factors must be weighed against the type and quantity of the defendant's contacts with the state.

Necessarily, then, the International Shoe standard as refined by the Supreme Court in its later decisions presents a fluid, policy oriented test, which requires a detailed analysis of the facts in order to decide what is just in each case. The standard applies to both individual and corporate defendants. Because of its flexibility, it allows the courts, in cases with individual defendants, t~ into account the extra burdens that may · broad extensions of jurisdiction, ~·᠎ specialized rules for any part᠎

§ 2–17. Applica᠎
        T᠎

The᠎
tacts n᠎
threshol᠎
contacts, v᠎
factors, wil᠎
only imprecis᠎
within the dis᠎
less, some exai᠎
considerations tha᠎

If a corporation or an individual is continuously and systematically entering the state and the cause of action arises out of those in-state activities, then jurisdiction is proper. International Shoe Co. v. Washington (S.Ct.1945). Not only are the contacts substantial, but also the forum usually will be convenient for all concerned as the witnesses, evidence, and governing law will be there. This also may be true when the cause of action arises outside the state, but out of activities that occurred within the state. Cornelison v. Chaney (Cal.1976). At the opposite end of the spectrum, if the defendant's contacts are only sporadic and the cause of action does not arise out of them, whether it arises within or without the state, minimum contacts will not be found and jurisdiction will not be allowed regardless of the convenience of the forum. Hanson v. Denckla (S.Ct.1958). In cases that fall between these two extremes, the decision whether there are sufficient minimum contacts will depend largely on balancing the fairness of the forum against the quality and ntity of the contacts the defendant has had with state.

Supreme Court in a 1984 decision, Helicopte-
onales de Colombia, S.A. v. Hall (S.Ct.
ressed these cases, recognizing a distinc-
actions in which "general jurisdic-
ed and those in which "specific juris-
g invoked. The former embrace
which the defendant has engaged
forum related activity but the
not arise out of that conduct;

the latter involve cases in which the defendant's activity in the forum is sporadic but the cause of action arises out of those dealings. In order to assert general jurisdiction, the court must be able to find substantial forum activity by the defendant and thus the threshold for satisfying minimum contacts in that situation is much greater than in specific jurisdiction cases. Examples best illustrate how these distinctions may work.

Specific jurisdiction has been upheld based on a single act of the defendant, such as in the case of nonresident motorists who have an auto accident in the forum state, causing an injury there. Or, cases involving a contract dispute in which the contract involved is the only one into which the defendant has entered. In the former case, the interest of the state in providing a forum for its resident plaintiff and regulating its highways coupled with the fact that the defendant purposefully entered the state, and the convenience of the forum insofar as the evidence is concerned, permits the assertion of jurisdiction consistent with notions of fair play. Hess v. Pawloski (S.Ct.1927). In the latter situation, the type of contract involved, the amount of activities the defendant undertook in the state in connection with the contract, and a finding that the defendant purposefully entered the state in order to make the contract may justify the assertion of jurisdiction even when only a single contract is involved. McGee v. International Life Ins. Co. (S.Ct.1957)(insurance contract).

However, in contract disputes the decision whether the International Shoe standard has been met in single act cases often requires a very complex inquiry. Thus, the Supreme Court has noted that in contract actions it is not appropriate to determine jurisdiction by attempting to identify an artificial locus of the contract. Rather, the question whether minimum contacts are satisfied depends upon an inquiry into the facts surrounding the prior negotiations and their contemplated future consequences, the terms of the contract, and the parties actual course of dealing. Burger King Corp. v. Rudzewicz (S.Ct.1985). Further, the presumptions relied upon in tort cases to support jurisdiction regarding the burdensomeness on the defendant, the interest of the state in the issue in dispute, and the convenience of the forum may be inappropriate in a contract action. Thus, the court may take into account the fact that a resident seller induced the buyer into the contract and into the jurisdiction, or that the plaintiff is a major corporation that has easy access to another more convenient forum and the defendant is an individual for whom it will be very burdensome to defend in the forum state.

In cases in which the cause of action is unrelated to defendant's continuous activities within the forum but it occurs within that state, general jurisdiction may be proper depending on other factors indicating the fairness of the forum. For example, jurisdiction was allowed in a products liability suit when the defendant manufacturer sent many of its products into the state even though the product at issue in the case was not part of those that the defendant sent into the jurisdiction. Buckeye Boiler Co. v. Superior Court of Los Angeles County (Cal.1969). The key factors supporting jurisdiction were the minimal potential burden on the defendant in having to defend in the forum, the convenience of the forum in terms of the witnesses and evidence, and the difficulty for the plaintiff if forced to seek an alternative forum.

On the other hand, if the cause of action not only fails to arise out of the defendant's activities in the forum state, but also arises outside the state, then general jurisdiction may be denied because the assertion of jurisdiction would not be sufficiently fair, despite the defendant's other unrelated continuous activities in the state. Helicopteros Nacionales de Colombia, S.A. v. Hall (S.Ct.1984). Thus, the fact that defendant sent some of its products regularly into California was not deemed enough to sustain in personam jurisdiction over a claim for an injury caused in Iowa by a product sent to Iowa. Fisher Governor Co. v. Superior Court (Cal.1959). However, it has been held that jurisdiction is proper in such a situation when the product was one purchased from the stream of commerce in the forum state. Singer v. Walker (N.Y.1965). These cases, again, depend on a close consideration of all the factors bearing on the interest of the state in providing a forum and the relative burdens placed on all the parties should jurisdiction be allowed or denied.

Another factor that may influence whether the assertion of jurisdiction comports with notions of fair play and substantial justice is whether the defendant is a nonresident alien. In Asahi Metal Industry Co. v. Superior Court (S.Ct.1987), the Supreme Court unanimously held that the assertion of jurisdiction by the California state court over a Japanese valve manufacturer in a suit arising out of a motorcycle accident in California violated the fairness portion of the International Shoe standard. The Court focussed on the special burdens imposed on foreign defendants in having to defend in the United States courts and concluded that those burdens were not outweighed by minimal interests on the part of the plaintiff and the forum State in asserting jurisdiction. Thus, the application of the minimum contacts standard in the international field requires special attention to be given to the inconvenience that may be entailed.

Finally, it should be noted that even when suit is brought in a federal court or against an alien defendant, in the absence of a special federal statute, the assessment of whether sufficient minimum contacts exist does not involve a review of the defendant's nationwide contacts, but looks only to contacts related to the forum state. Omni Capital Int'l v. Rudolf Wolff & Co. (S.Ct.1987). This is because the statutory basis for the assertion of jurisdiction over the nonresident is a state long-arm statute (see §§ 2–10—2–11, above), and necessarily the state possesses sufficient power to assert jurisdiction only over persons or events legitimately within its regulatory sphere (i.e., geographical borders). A reference to defendant's nationwide, as opposed to forum state, contacts is permissible only if the statutory basis for asserting jurisdiction is a federal long-arm authorizing nationwide service of process (see § 2–12, above), or if the action arises under federal law and the defendant is not otherwise subject to the general jurisdiction of any state (see § 2–11, above).

§ 2–18. Minimum Contacts as Applied to In Rem and Quasi In Rem Cases

In 1977 the Supreme Court decided Shaffer v. Heitner (S.Ct.1977), and adopted minimum contacts, fair play and substantial justice as the constitutional standard governing in rem and quasi in rem jurisdiction. No longer is it sufficient to invoke jurisdiction successfully merely by attaching property in the forum state. State sovereignty is not a proper basis on which to rest jurisdiction, instead the focus is on whether the defendant's due process rights are infringed by the court's assertion of jurisdiction. A close look at how the Court applied due process to the facts of Shaffer helps to understand how the standard will operate in other cases.

The case was a shareholder derivative action brought in Delaware against a corporation, Greyhound, and several of its present and former officers and directors. The corporation was incorporated in Delaware, but its principal place of business was Arizona. None of the individual defendants resided in Delaware. Plaintiff alleged that the corporation, while under the guidance of the individual defendants, had engaged in some activities in Oregon that had resulted in damages and fines against it for violating the antitrust laws. Those damages and fines were to the ultimate detriment of the corporation and thus the plaintiff, as a shareholder, sought relief for the damage caused to the corporation by the individual defendants' authorization of the illegal activities. In order to obtain jurisdiction over the nonresident individuals, the plaintiff utilized the state sequestration statute and, invoking a Delaware law declaring the situs of all stock in Delaware corporations to be in that state, seized approximately 82,000 shares of stock belonging to the defendants by placing stop transfer orders on the books of the corporation. The lower Delaware courts upheld this assertion of quasi in rem jurisdiction, but the Supreme Court reversed.

Applying the International Shoe standard, the Court ruled that the presence of property in the state was not sufficient in and of itself. The cause of action was deemed not related to that property because the defendants' stock ownership was not directly tied to their fiduciary relationship to the corporation. Additional contacts were necessary. The Court noted that Delaware had not manifested any particular state interest in regulating the defendants' conduct by asserting jurisdiction over them because its sequestration statute was a general one, not designed specially for the regulation of its corporations and their officers. Finally, it concluded that even if Delaware had manifested a strong state interest and minimum contacts were established, Delaware was not a fair forum in which to hear the dispute. The individual defendants had never purposefully availed themselves of the opportunity to conduct activities in the state or had anything to do with the state. They had no reason to expect to be brought before a Delaware court since the ownership of stock could not be deemed to imply consent to suit in the state of incorporation. In addition, there was an alternative forum that would not be unfair; presumably the suit could be filed in Arizona, the principal place of business of Greyhound, or Oregon, where the allegedly illegal activity took place.

Although the Shaffer Court made clear that the mere presence of property in the forum no longer suffices to confer jurisdiction there, that fact is not irrelevant to a jurisdictional analysis. Rather, the presence of the property may suggest other contacts that are sufficient to permit jurisdiction to be exercised. In particular this is so when the property is directly related to plaintiff's claim for relief. For example, the utilization of the minimum contacts standard in pure in rem cases is not likely to have much effect on the decision to take jurisdiction. In typical in rem actions in which the subject matter of the action is the attached property itself, minimum contacts will be found. Most in rem cases involve real property, where the state's traditional interest in regulating all matters relating to its property is well recognized. Further, because of the tangible, immovable nature of the property, it will be clearly foreseeable to the defendant that jurisdiction might be asserted. The ownership of the property itself will demonstrate that the defendant benefitted from the protection of the laws of the state. Indeed, if land is attached in order to assert quasi in rem jurisdiction, the International Shoe standard also may be met as the type of contact the defendant has with the state may be viewed as so substantial that it would not be unfair to require the defendant to defend there, even on an unrelated cause of action.

As acknowledged by the Shaffer Court itself, the main impact of applying the International Shoe standard will be in those cases in which movable or intangible property is involved, or in which, as in Shaffer, the property is viewed as totally unrelated to the claims being asserted. The nature of the property may suggest that the defendant may not knowingly have entered the state or invoked the protection of its laws and that defendant's contact with the state is minimal. In these cases the jurisdictional decision must rest on a careful inquiry into the type of contacts the defendant has had with the state, the interest of the forum in the underlying controversy, whether the plaintiff has another forum available that might be more fair, and the actual burden on the defendant in having to litigate in the forum. Similarly, even if the property is secure in the state, it is necessary to find other ties between the defendant, the forum and the litigation before the assertion of jurisdiction will be deemed fair.

Applying the minimum contacts standard, it is quite clear that the attachment of a wandering debtor in order to reach another nonresident debtor, without more, no longer will be permissible. On the other hand, the difficulty in assessing the fairness concerns in less clear cases is exemplified by the fact that for a few years after Shaffer there was some dispute over whether quasi in rem jurisdiction could be asserted in suits brought against a nonresident tortfeasor through the attachment of the defendant's insurance policy. Those courts upholding jurisdiction focused on three things: (1) the insurance company was clearly doing business in the forum state and actually would be the one conducting the defense of the action; (2) the interest of the state in providing a forum for its injured resident; and (3) the protection afforded the named defendant by allowing a limited appearance restricting defendant's potential liability to the insurance coverage. The Supreme Court ended speculation in 1980, overruling this form of attachment jurisdiction and applying a straightforward minimum contacts analysis to strike down jurisdiction. Rush v. Savchuk (S.Ct.1980).

§ 2–19. Current Utility of the Three Jurisdictional Categories

Although the minimum contacts standard must be applied to all types of jurisdiction, the tripartite division of jurisdiction into in rem, quasi in rem, and in personam still serves some useful purposes. On a purely practical level, it is a useful device to identify what is in issue and what contacts may be most relevant. Illustratively, in the pure in rem suit an analysis of whether the facts of the case fit the traditional quiet title pattern typically will demonstrate simultaneously that the constitutional standard has been met.

Quasi in rem jurisdiction also remains a separate and useful jurisdictional category on a much more important level. In those states that do not have long-arm statutes authorizing the assertion of extraterritorial jurisdiction to the furthest constitutional limits, the plaintiff's case may not fit within the specific categories set out in the statute. Even though sufficient minimum contacts could be found to meet due process concerns, the absence of an applicable long-arm statute prohibits the assertion of in personam jurisdiction. If an attachment statute exists and the defendant owns some property that is in the state, however, quasi in rem jurisdiction will be permissible.

Finally, the threshold for establishing minimum contacts also may differ depending on the type of jurisdiction that is being asserted. In quasi in rem actions the judgment is limited to the value of the property, and, in many instances, the defendant will be allowed to enter and defend on the merits without submitting to the in personam jurisdiction of the court. (See § 2–28, below.) These added protections for the defendant, coupled with a finding of the forum state's regulatory interest in the controversy, may support a conclusion that a particular forum meets the International Shoe standard for quasi in rem jurisdiction purposes, even though there are not enough contacts to support the assertion of in personam jurisdiction. It must be remembered that the Shaffer Court emphasized that in evaluating the minimum contacts standard the trial court should focus on the ties between the defendant, the forum, and the litigation, thereby allowing consideration of the forum state's interest in the litigation to be weighed in determining whether jurisdiction can be asserted. In contrast, when in personam jurisdiction is invoked, the Court has emphasized that only the relationship between the defendant and the forum state is relevant in determining whether the threshold minimum contacts are present; the forum state's interest is relevant only later when considering whether fair play and substantial justice are satisfied. See § 2–16, above.

§ 2–20. Current Viability of Consent, Domicile and Transient Jurisdiction Theories

Given the sweeping language in Shaffer v. Heitner to the effect that all forms of jurisdiction must meet the International Shoe standard, some questions can be raised about the current viability of some of the other traditional bases of jurisdiction that do not rest on a minimum contacts analysis. In particular, can jurisdiction continue to be premised on the defendant's consent, domicile or transient presence in the forum state without any additional contacts?

In the case of jurisdiction resting on consent or domicile, the answer is clearly yes. The Supreme Court's invocation of minimum contacts is for the purpose of establishing constitutional limits on the states' assertions of jurisdiction—essentially the standard balances the rights of the forum state and the defendant and suggests when defendants legitimately may object to defending in a particular forum. But the defendant need not object if the defendant does not want to. Thus the right of defendant to consent to jurisdiction is not incompatible with the Shaffer Court's pronouncements.

For different reasons jurisdiction premised on defendant's domicile also remains constitutional. The premise of domicile jurisdiction is that it always is fair to make a person amenable to suit where she is domiciled—the very determination of domicile suggests that defendant has some continuing and permanent ties to the state and thus could foresee being sued there. Although there may be cases today in which an individual may be changing domiciles and the invocation of the traditional rule might seem unfair, in the vast majority of cases, domicile will remain a sufficient contact on which to base jurisdiction.

The traditional form of jurisdiction that seems most incompatible with the minimum contacts approach is that premised on the mere transient presence of the defendant. Transient jurisdiction rests on the territoriality principles espoused in Pennoyer v. Neff and the state's sovereign power over all persons and things within its borders. After Shaffer, those principles generally were viewed as rejected. Thus, although the temporary physical presence of a person within the forum is a contact with the state, in the absence of any other contacts between the defendant, the forum and the litigation, the propriety of jurisdiction in those cases was questioned.

The Supreme Court addressed the continued viability of transient jurisdiction in Burnham v. Superior Court (S.Ct.1990), unanimously upholding California's assertion of jurisdiction over a New Jersey resident who was served with process in a divorce action while in the state to conduct business and visit his children. The justices did not all agree as to why due process was satisfied, however. Some found it sufficient to rely on the strong history and tradition supporting transient jurisdiction, and others determined that the in-state service rule satisfied fairness standards. Thus, it now is clear that tagging the defendant in the forum state, without more, remains a legitimate and constitutional means of obtaining jurisdiction over nonresident defendants.

3. OTHER JURISDICTIONAL CONSTRAINTS

§ 2–21. Notice

Although a case meets both the statutory and constitutional requirements for personal jurisdiction, the suit may be dismissed or the judgment collaterally attacked if insufficient notice is given to the defendant. The defendant can claim that the proceeding violated due process because without proper notice there was no effective opportunity to be heard. What constitutes proper notice so as to satisfy the constitution involves an inquiry into both the type of notice utilized and the timing of the notice. The latter element ensures that the opportunity to be heard is a realistic one and is discussed in § 6–4, below. The type of notice goes to the heart of whether a defendant has any opportunity to defend at all.

In in personam cases, individual service of process clearly is the best means of ensuring actual notice and thus a favored way of obtaining jurisdiction. Similarly, although the historic rule in in rem proceedings was that attachment of the property plus publication was a sufficient means of notifying the defendant, the modern rule is that individual notice must be sent when the identity and location of the defendant is known. Walker v. City of Hutchison (S.Ct.1956).

Individual notice is not a constitutional prerequisite to all actions; the type of notice that must be utilized is decided on a case by case basis. The key in all cases, regardless of the type of jurisdiction involved, is what is practicable, with the emphasis on utilizing the means of notice that is most likely to reach the defendant. When determining what type of notice to require, the court also may consider the difficulties (cost, as well as impracticability) of locating the defendant and the need for the adjudication. Mullane v. Central Hanover Bank &

Trust Co. (S.Ct.1950). Applying this standard, the Supreme Court has held that if the defendant's address may be ascertained by reasonably diligent efforts, publication will not suffice and individual notice must be utilized. Tulsa Professional Collection Servs., Inc. v. Pope (S.Ct.1988); Mennonite Bd. of Missions v. Adams (S.Ct.1983). Posting notice on residential property rather than using first-class mail also has been deemed insufficient when mailed notice was more likely to reach the defendant. Greene v. Lindsey (S.Ct.1982).

Finally, although the defendant may attack a judgment on the ground that insufficient notice was given, a defect in the mere formalities or techniques of giving notice will not render the judgment constitutionally suspect. (See § 2–31, below.) Further, a party always can waive his rights to notice by contract. National Equipment Rental, Ltd. v. Szukhent (S.Ct.1964). In the absence of some evidence that the waiver was not knowing or voluntary, it will not be deemed violative of due process. D.H. Overmyer Co. v. Frick Co. (S.Ct.1972)(waiver to jurisdiction, notice, and service of process deemed constitutional).

§ 2–22. Other Constitutional Limits

Most of the decisions in the area of personal jurisdiction have involved an elaboration of the meaning of due process as contained in the minimum contacts standard and as required to provide adequate notice and an opportunity to be heard. However, a few other constitutional limits on what otherwise would be a proper exercise of jurisdiction have been suggested.

An essential element of due process is the notion that the court before whom the parties are appearing has the power to assure that once a judgment is rendered the defendant will not be subject to double or multiple liability in another court. If the court cannot provide this assurance, and an alternative forum exists where all the interested parties can be joined, then the suit must be dismissed on the defendant's motion even though all other jurisdictional prerequisites are met. For example, a Pennsylvania action to escheat funds held by Western Union as uncollected money orders was dismissed when the Pennsylvania court could not obtain jurisdiction over all the other states that also might claim the funds and thus could not protect the defendant against subsequent liability to those states for the same funds. An alternate forum, the Supreme Court, was available and could provide this protection. Western Union Tel. Co. v. Pennsylvania (S.Ct.1961).

A serious problem is presented when no forum exists in which all interested litigants may be joined. The Supreme Court has ruled that the desire to protect the defendant from multiple liability does not permit the court to bind absent persons to a judgment, if they are not otherwise within the court's personal jurisdiction reach. If personal jurisdiction is not obtained over those absent parties, then the defendant may suffer having to pay twice. New York Life Ins. Co. v. Dunlevy (S.Ct.1916). In order to avoid this occurrence, some courts have applied the minimum contacts standard so as to stretch their personal jurisdiction reach to ensure that all the pertinent parties are before the court. See, e.g., Atkinson v. Superior Court (Cal.1957). Notice requirements also have been construed in a more flexible manner when to require individual notice would prevent the suit from being maintained and there is no alternative means of settling as a final matter defendant's potential liability. See, e.g., Mullane v. Central Hanover Bank & Trust Co. (S.Ct.1950).

A few lower courts have relied on the interstate commerce clause as a separate limitation on the exercise of extraterritorial jurisdiction by a state. An attempted assertion of jurisdiction was held to have a direct and negative impact on interstate commerce—discouraging it because of a liberal long-arm statute. Thus, jurisdiction was denied even though the forum appeared to be a fair one under a due process standard. Erlanger Mills, Inc. v. Cohoes Fibre Mills, Inc. (4th Cir.1956). A majority of courts have not adopted this standard, however, and it has not had any significant impact on the expansion of personal jurisdiction.

Some lower courts also invoked the First Amendment to limit assertions of jurisdiction in libel actions against nonresident publishers. E.g., New York Times Co. v. Connor (5th Cir.1966). These courts held that a higher than ordinary threshold of minimum contacts had to be crossed in these libel actions because of the danger that forcing the publishers to defend in a distant and inconvenient forum could have a chilling effect on free speech. The Supreme Court subsequently made it clear, however, that First Amendment concerns are not properly part of the jurisdictional inquiry. Calder v. Jones (S.Ct.1984).

Thus, jurisdiction limitations arising out of constitutional clauses other than Due Process have not really developed. Rather, the Supreme Court has restricted jurisdiction primarily through additional refinements to its minimum contacts standard.

4. SERVICE OF PROCESS—THE MEANS OF ASSERTING JURISDICTION

§ 2–23. Types of Service

Local statutes of the state in which suit is brought determine what type of service may be authorized in the state courts. Federal Rule 4 sets out the general rules governing how federal process is served, and it also authorizes the federal courts to make use of any applicable state law methods. Fed. Rule 4(e)(1). Federal courts may utilize the procedure set out in state long-arm statutes, or in state attachment statutes in actions based on quasi in rem jurisdiction. Special rules are provided in Federal Rule 4(f) and in treaties with specific countries as to how service is to be accomplished outside United States borders.

In general there are three types of service—actual, substituted and constructive. When actual service is utilized, in-hand delivery of the summons and complaint is made. In the case of a corporate or governmental defendant, the statutes frequently denominate the person who is authorized to receive actual service. For corporations this often is the company's general or managing agent, (Fed.Rule 4(h)(1)), for governments it may be a designated official, such as the United States attorney in the district in which suit is brought (Fed.Rule 4(i)).

Substituted service embraces a wide variety of means of notifying the defendant of the action without personal delivery of the summons and complaint. Most state long-arm statutes, for example, provide for process to be sent to the defendant by registered mail. Attachment statutes also provide a means of substituted service in that they typically authorize the seizure of the property, with notice being mailed to the owner. More directly, the defendant may denominate an in-state person to receive actual process, with mailed notice being sent to him. Process also may be delivered to the defendant's dwelling house and left with a person "of suitable age and discretion." (Fed.Rule 4(e)(2)). Finally, in an effort to avoid costs associated with service, Federal Rule 4(d)(2) provides a procedure by which the plaintiff can simply notify the defendant of the commencement of the action and request the defendant to waive service of a summons. If the defendant does not comply with the request and cannot show good cause for that failure, the court will impose the costs incurred in effecting service.

Constructive service,—service by publication—historically was the primary means of service of process on out-of-state defendants in in rem jurisdiction cases. Since the main purpose of service of process is to ensure that the defendant is notified of the action, constructive service now may be permitted only when other more direct means of notice, such as mailing, are not possible. McDonald v. Mabee (S.Ct.1917). If the defendant's whereabouts are unknown, and there is no domicile to which process can be delivered, then service by publication may be allowed. See Cal.Civ.Proc.Code § 415.50.

§ 2–24. Impermissible Use of Service

In general the courts have allowed process servers to employ whatever means necessary to complete personal service on recalcitrant defendants. However, if the means used not only induced the defendant to accept service, but also enticed the defendant into the jurisdiction and the only basis for the court's personal jurisdiction is service in the state, then the suit may be dismissed. Further, if a default judgment is entered, it may be collaterally attacked on the ground that jurisdiction was obtained by fraud. Although this challenge does not involve a constitutional defect in the original judgment, it is upheld because the courts will not validate jurisdiction that is obtained by improper or false means.

§ 2–25. Immunity From Process

There are certain circumstances when service of process cannot be effectuated on a potential defen-

dant who is within the state. I...
active participation in judicial pro...
have full and fair trials, the courts ...
granted immunity from process to all tri...
pants who otherwise would be outside the ...
jurisdictional reach. The one exception to this r...
is in the case of counterclaims against a nonresident
plaintiff. Immunity is not given in that situation
because, by instituting the action, the plaintiff has
submitted to the court's jurisdiction. Immunity
protects nonresident attorneys, parties, and witnesses from being served with process in an unrelated action while in attendance or in transit to a
trial, criminal or civil, within the state. It also has
been extended to cover persons who were within the
state for the sole purpose of discussing an out-of-
court settlement.

Since immunity from process is premised on a
desire to encourage nonresidents to enter the state
voluntarily when they otherwise could remain outside, it does not apply if the potential defendant
entered the state before any action was brought but
subsequently was detained involuntarily and then
served with process. Similarly, the doctrine is of no
utility if the person is subject to the extraterritorial
long-arm jurisdiction of the court as the defendant
cannot prevent service merely by staying outside
the state's borders. Thus, with the great expansion
of long-arm jurisdiction in recent years, immunity
from process has become a doctrine of decreasing
utility for parties, although it still may play an
important role for witnesses.

AINTIFF'S

CK

diction

ter jurisdiction ad-
or statutory power
oversy, they involve
nature of the court
personal right. Thus,
an obje̶c̶ er jurisdiction can be
made at any tim̶e ̶ ̶ ̶ ̶ ̶ ̶ ut the proceedings; it
even may be raised for the first time on appeal.
Consistent with this flexibility, a party may raise
this defense either in the responsive pleading or by
a separate motion to dismiss (Fed.Rule 12(b)). Further, the court has an independent obligation to
inquire into its subject-matter jurisdiction and may
raise any issues relating thereto sua sponte at the
trial or appellate level. In sum, there are no real
restrictions on raising a subject-matter defense during the course of the proceedings to which the
objection is being made.

§ 2–27. Personal Jurisdiction

Because issues of personal jurisdiction are tied to
the personal due process rights of the defendant,
the defendant can waive objections to the court's
power over him. Consent to jurisdiction may occur
prior to any suit being filed, see § 2–15, above.
After an action is brought, however, except in the
rare circumstance in which the defendant makes a

75

formal statement waiving all personal jurisdiction objections, it is necessary to establish some means by which the court can ascertain when the defendant has participated in the proceedings to such a degree that it would be appropriate to hold that he impliedly has waived any objections and consents to jurisdiction. The method commonly used is to establish special rules governing how defendants can object to personal jurisdiction. The failure to comply with the procedures established constitutes consent.

One method of challenging the court's personal jurisdiction is by special appearance. Many states require a defendant who wishes to object to personal jurisdiction to enter a "special appearance" prior to answering on the merits. In order to preserve this objection, the defendant typically is not permitted to introduce any other defenses at that time or prior to making the special appearance. If the defendant does so, he will be deemed to have made a general appearance and to have waived the right to object to jurisdiction. The sole exception involves objections to the court's subject-matter jurisdiction; the defendant may join objections to the subject-matter jurisdiction of the court with personal jurisdiction objections without making a general appearance.

If, when ruling on defendant's jurisdiction objection, the court finds that personal jurisdiction does not exist, the suit will be dismissed. However, if it rules against the defendant, then the question presented is whether the defendant waives the right to object on appeal by continuing to defend on the merits. In states allowing appeals only from final judgments, the defendant has preserved his objection by making the initial special appearance and may raise the objection anew on a direct appeal from the final judgment on the merits. In other states that provide for some sort of interlocutory appeal, the defendant waives the objection by failing immediately to appeal the court's ruling before defending on the merits and, in that event, will not be allowed to raise the jurisdiction issue on an appeal from the final judgment. In either case, once the defendant enters a special appearance and receives an adverse ruling, the only means of obtaining further review is by a direct appeal; the defendant cannot subsequently default and attempt to collaterally attack the judgment on personal jurisdiction grounds. See § 2–31, below.

The distinction between general and special appearances has been abolished in the federal courts and in those states that have adopted the federal rules. Instead of requiring the defendant to make a special appearance in order to object to personal jurisdiction, the defendant may raise the objection either in a pretrial motion to dismiss or in the answer, Fed.Rule 12(b). Further, other objections may be raised at the same time. The defendant's options are circumscribed primarily by timing constraints. The failure to include a personal jurisdiction defense in a pretrial motion raising other defenses, Fed.Rule 12(g), or to include the defense in the answer when no pretrial motions have been made, Fed.Rule 12(h)(1), will result in the total waiver of the defense. As in the case of a special appearance, once a timely objection has been made, it may be raised again on a direct appeal, but it cannot be the basis for a collateral attack.

§ 2–28. Limited Appearances

In actions based on quasi in rem jurisdiction, special problems have arisen because of a desire to give the defendant an opportunity to protect the property seized without forcing the defendant to submit to the court's in personam jurisdiction. A number of states adopted the device of a limited appearance in response to this problem. In those states, the defendant by making a limited appearance can defend the action on the merits; if he loses, only the property will be forfeited; if he wins, no binding effect will be given to the judgment so the plaintiff may sue again in another court in which jurisdiction may be obtained. In states not authorizing a limited appearance, a defendant faced with a proper quasi in rem action has two options: (1) he can default and thereby forfeit the property, or (2) he can enter to defend on the merits and thereby submit to the court's in personam jurisdiction. Which option is preferable will depend on the value of the attached property as compared to the amount of damages being sought by the plaintiff.

The federal rules do not address the propriety of limited appearances. Thus, in actions brought in the federal courts the availability of the procedure depends on whether the court refers to state law as

the governing law on that issue. See § 9–2, below.
Because courts are split on the propriety of making
a limited appearance (with the slightly more prevalent view allowing it), it is most important to check
the local law where the action is brought to determine its availability.

Perhaps because of the seeming wastefulness of a
second trial when the first was fully litigated, a few
courts have suggested that binding effect should be
given to the specific issues actually decided in the
first quasi in rem action. However, giving even this
limited binding effect to the judgment effectively
treats it as in personam, to the detriment of the
defendant. Thus, this approach is somewhat controversial.

The utility of the limited appearance as a major
protection against the seeming harshness of quasi
in rem jurisdiction clearly has decreased. As discussed earlier, it now is clear that this form of
jurisdiction must be premised on more than the
mere presence of property within the forum state;
the court must find that the assertion of jurisdiction, even of this limited scope, satisfies the minimum contacts and fair play and substantial justice
criteria. See § 2–18, above. Consequently, the
availability of a limited appearance no longer is the
sole safeguard against unfairness to a defendant in
a quasi in rem action.

§ 2–29. Venue and Service of Process

Objections to the court's venue or the means or
form of service of process must be made at the

outset of the action or they will be waived. This is true because both venue and service of process involve concerns of a less important nature than those underlying subject-matter or personal jurisdiction. Since venue restrictions are designed primarily to identify a convenient forum, the failure of the defendant to raise the lack of venue either in a pretrial motion to dismiss or in the answer will be deemed acquiescence. Indeed, in many instances the remedy for improper venue is not dismissal, but transfer, see § 2–30, below. Service of process objections that do not involve the failure to give actual notice or to obtain personal jurisdiction present primarily technical problems dealing with the form or method of process. Defects of that character are waivable unless raised by pretrial motion or in the answer. Further, although it is important to comply with the statutory requirements for service of process, the court often will not dismiss the action if the defect can be corrected by amending the process. Thus, most commonly, motions to quash service or to dismiss because of improper service are joined with motions to dismiss based on a lack of personal jurisdiction. When filed alone, they frequently are dilatory tactics.

§ 2–30. Forum Non Conveniens and Transfer

There are circumstances in which although the forum chosen by the plaintiff meets venue requirements, a better, more convenient forum exists. In recognition of this fact, the judicial doctrine of *forum non conveniens* developed, under which the defendant may make a motion to dismiss the action, even though the plaintiff's choice of forum meets all statutory and constitutional requirements. The motion is addressed to the court's discretion and will be granted only infrequently, typically when the plaintiff's forum is clearly inconvenient and an alternative forum exists that is a vast improvement. In several states a forum non dismissal is not allowed whenever the plaintiff or one of the parties is a resident of the forum state. In some states, the doctrine has been abandoned altogether. However, in most instances no single factor will authorize or preclude dismissal as long as an alternative forum exists. There is a strong presumption to honor plaintiff's forum choice, but the court will balance against that presumption any factors relating to the convenience to all the parties, as well as to the judicial system, in determining whether to honor plaintiff's forum choice or grant a forum non dismissal. See Piper Aircraft Co. v. Reyno (S.Ct.1981). Further, the presumption is much weaker if a foreign plaintiff is involved. Finally, in order to protect the plaintiff, a court granting the motion often will do so only on condition that the defendant consent to suit in the alternative forum.

In the federal court system and within several states, forum non conveniens has been codified in a transfer statute. See 28 U.S.C.A. § 1404. These statutes permit the court to transfer the case to another court within the same system where it might have been brought. Thus, the transferee forum also must meet jurisdiction and venue requirements. Unlike what occurs on a forum non motion, however, either party may move to transfer, and they need not dismiss and then recommence the action. Indeed, the court can transfer a case on its own motion. Transfer often may be obtained on a lesser showing of inconvenience than would be necessary if a forum non motion were presented. Nonetheless, even in those systems having transfer statutes, forum non conveniens remains an important tool since transfers are limited to courts within the same system. If the defendant wants to change from a federal forum to a court in another country or from one state court to the state courts in another state, a motion to dismiss for forum non conveniens is the appropriate method.

One further difference between forum non conveniens and transfer should be noted. Forum non conveniens is premised on the fact that both the original court and some other court meet all the applicable jurisdiction and venue requirements. Although transfer can be only to a court in which the action could have been brought, special statutory provisions in the federal system permit transfer when the original forum had no venue to a court where venue is proper. 28 U.S.C.A. § 1406(a). In addition, the Supreme Court has upheld a transfer when the transferor court had no personal jurisdiction and the statute of limitations had run so that to dismiss the suit for lack of jurisdiction would have resulted in forfeiting the claim. Goldlawr, Inc. v. Heiman (S.Ct.1962). This application of the transfer statute typically has been restricted to situations in which the lack of personal jurisdiction was not clear at the outset, so that dismissal would be unduly harsh to the plaintiff.

2.   COLLATERAL ATTACK

§ 2–31.   Principles Governing

When a defendant interposes an objection to the plaintiff's choice of the forum in action A in an action to enforce the judgment obtained in A, or in some other proceeding before another trial court, B, this is called a collateral attack on the judgment in A.   The availability of collateral attack is severely restricted because it erodes the finality and stability of judgments.   In situations in which action B is in a different court system than A, it violates statutory, 28 U.S.C.A. § 1738, and constitutional principles, Art. IV, § 1, providing that full faith and credit should be given to sister state judgments. Thus, collateral attack may be available only when the type of objection the defendant raises is of a constitutional dimension;   venue objections being merely matters of convenience or service of process objections that involve merely the form of the service never can be raised on collateral attack.

The following rules apply to determine when a collateral attack is permitted as a means of raising a subject-matter or personal jurisdiction defense.   If the defendant never appears in action A and a default judgment is entered, then the judgment may be collaterally attacked on either ground.   If the defendant appears and raises the jurisdiction objections, fully litigating them in the trial court in A, then collateral attack is barred; defendant's only remedy is a direct attack on appeal.

Special rules apply if the defendant appears in A and defends on the merits without ever challenging either the court's subject-matter jurisdiction or its personal jurisdiction. If defendant fails to raise any objections to personal jurisdiction, collateral attack is not available to later raise the defense. The personal jurisdiction defense was waived by the failure to make a timely objection. See § 2–27, above. The problem of whether to allow collateral attack on subject-matter jurisdiction grounds when the defendant has fully participated in the first proceeding, but failed to raise any objection there, is more complicated because parties cannot consent to the subject-matter jurisdiction of the court. The few cases that have considered the problem suggest that typically collateral attack will not be available. However, if the policy against the court's acting beyond its jurisdiction is strong, such as when a state court improperly hears matters confined to the exclusive jurisdiction of the federal courts, or when the jurisdictional defect raises problems of sovereign immunity, then a collateral attack may be permitted. Additionally, the court may consider whether the jurisdiction determination depends on a question of law rather than fact or whether the lack of subject-matter jurisdiction was clear. These and other factors designed to aid in balancing the conflicting policies of finality and limited jurisdiction are suggested in Section 10 of the *Restatement Second of Judgments* (1982).

CHAPTER III

PRETRIAL: FRAMING THE LITIGATION

A. PLEADING

§ 3–1. General Theory of Pleading

The pleadings are the papers by which the litigants first set the case before the court. A thorough study of the art of pleading embraces both procedural and substantive concerns. *How* you plead is a procedural question, depending on the specific rules of the court in which you are appearing. *What* you plead is determined by considerations of substantive law and the knowledge of what facts are legally significant in each context. The primary focus in this book is on the first question. For a more detailed discussion of the art of pleading, see J. Friedenthal, M. Kane & A. Miller, *Civil Procedure*, Ch. 5 (2d ed.1993).

There have been four historic functions associated with pleading: (1) notice giving; (2) fact revelation; (3) issue formulation; and (4) screening to constrict or expand the flow of litigation in a particular court system. Different procedural systems rely on the pleadings for one or a combination of these purposes. Depending on which of these functions is emphasized, more or less detail may be required and a given pleading may be deemed sufficient or insufficient and subject to dismissal. Thus, it is important to understand the philosophy underlying the pleading system for the court in which suit is brought in order to better understand the level of specificity or degree of flexibility that exists.

§ 3–2. History: Common Law Pleading

Although it is virtually nonexistent in American courts today, common law pleading is the direct antecedent of modern code and federal rule pleading and is important to consider in order to better evaluate the present pleading rules. Pleading in common law courts was characterized by rigid formality and precision; its object was to produce through the pleadings a single issue for trial. A plaintiff could plead only a single cause of action (claim) in a given case and the defendant could make only one response. Alternative or multiple defenses were not permitted. The failure to comply with the pleading rules resulted in the dismissal of the action, with no leave to replead. Thus, the course of pleading was perilous and great attention was given to that portion of the proceedings because the pleadings truly acted as a screening device, preventing many cases from going forward. Suits in equity courts were not governed by the same rigid, complex system. Since those proceedings were solely before a judge, joinder of claims and parties was allowed, some discovery was available, and the pleadings did not act as the primary screening device.

A brief description of how common law pleading operated illustrates its formality, as well as pitfalls. In order to bring an action, the plaintiff had to determine which of the existing forms of action best suited the facts of his case and obtain the proper writ (summons) for that form of action. Examples of the historic forms of action are detinue, debt, replevin, covenant, trespass, and trespass on the case. The forms of action were essentially categories of legal liability; if no form of action existed to meet plaintiff's needs, there was no remedy for the alleged wrong. The use of an improper writ for the wrong alleged resulted in a dismissal with prejudice. Defense counsel were faced with a similar array of carefully defined responses. Defendant could: (1) deny that the facts if true gave plaintiff a legal right to relief (a demurrer); (2) enter a dilatory plea challenging plaintiff's right to have the case heard by the court before whom it was lodged; or (3) enter a plea in bar, denying that the alleged facts were true (a traverse) or arguing that even if the facts were true, other facts rendered the right unenforceable (confession and avoidance). These alternatives were mutually exclusive, even though they are not necessarily contradictory. If defendant pleaded in confession and avoidance, no issue was joined on the facts and the plaintiff had to respond to the newly introduced facts by demurrer, traverse, or another confession and avoidance. The exchange of pleadings continued until a single issue remained for trial.

As time passed, the common law pleading system became encrusted with requirements so that actions were won or lost not on the merits, but due to pleading niceties. The desire to produce a single, clear issue for trial became outweighed by the need to develop a system more responsive to the needs of the parties and less filled with pitfalls for the unwary. These feelings underlay the development of state pleading codes and ultimately federal rule pleading.

1. PLAINTIFF

§ 3–3. The Complaint: Code Pleading

Following the lead of New York, which adopted the Field Code in 1848, several states enacted statutes to govern the procedures in their courts. The pleading requirements included in those statutes commonly are referred to as code pleading.

Code pleading abolished the forms of action and eradicated much of the extreme formality and resulting pitfalls of common law pleading. The pleading distinctions between cases at law and those in equity were eliminated and a uniform set of pleading rules were adopted for all actions, regardless of the nature of the substantive cause of action. The function of the pleadings was transformed from one of issue formulation to fact revelation. Under code pleading, it typically is said that the plaintiff has only to plead the facts constituting a cause of action; in other words the plaintiff must plead the facts showing a legal right and wrong. If the allegations fit into some pattern of an established right, the case can continue. This standard is designed to provide notice to the opposing party, as well as to give the court sufficient information to allow it to strike or dismiss legally insufficient claims and avoid useless trials.

The plaintiff can plead alternatively and even inconsistently, at least when the facts are not all within her knowledge, as long as the pleading is in good faith. The only restraint on alternative allegations is that they must be placed in separate counts so as to give adequate notice to the defendant. Multiple causes of action may be alleged, as long as they too are placed in separate counts.

Although the rigid formality of the common law has been abandoned under the codes, fact pleading presents its own problems. First, there has been some difficulty in defining what constitutes a cause of action. Two different views prevail. One, called the primary rights theory, defines the cause of action in terms of the nature of the injury allegedly suffered. The focus is on the harm caused rather than the acts that produced the harm or the remedy; the pleader must set forth only all the facts showing each injury. The other view defines a cause of action by the events that give rise to a right to relief and requires the pleader to set forth the "aggregate of operative facts" for which relief is demanded. Difficulty in applying these two views arises because under the primary rights approach courts do not always agree as to what constitutes a single harm, and under the operative facts approach there is no focus provided to determine what facts may be sufficiently related, creating the potential for long and complex pleadings.

Another problem under code pleading is determining the level of detailed facts that must be pleaded. It usually has been said that the plaintiff need plead only ultimate facts, not evidentiary facts or legal conclusions. Attempts to delineate the difference between these three terms fill the case reports. In practice, the distinction is primarily one of how much detail is involved. Thus, ultimate facts are those essential to show that the plaintiff has a cause of action. Under a theory of cause of action as the breach of a primary right, the plaintiff must allege a primary right possessed by him, a corresponding duty on the defendant and the facts showing a wrong by the defendant constituting a breach. Any special damages also must be alleged. Evidentiary facts provide greater detail and legal conclusions are necessarily more general and vague. The pleading of evidentiary facts, while improper, generally is harmless and will not result in dismissal. However, a pleading that is filled only with legal conclusions will be fatally defective.

The use of the common counts in some contract cases also is authorized under code pleading, providing an exception to the normal degree of specificity that is required. Under the common counts the pleader need allege only that he is suing for unjust enrichment (money had and received), for labor performed (quantum valebant) or for goods sold and delivered or services rendered but not paid for (quantum meruit). No further facts need be alleged. Thus, in an action based on a common count, there is much less emphasis on the pleadings; indeed, so much so that the common counts remain somewhat anomalous in the code pleading system. The best explanation for the tolerance of this vague pleading standard is that the type of action involved is really one for restitution, premised on a desire to prevent the defendant from being unjustly enriched. Consequently, an action based on the common counts is equitable in nature and historically did not fall within the common law pleading system.

§ 3–4. The Complaint: Federal ("Notice") Pleading

The most liberal pleading system is that utilized in the federal courts and in the many state courts that have adopted the federal rules. Under the federal system, notice pleading prevails with the sole concern being whether the complaint reveals enough information so that the defendant can respond and understand why he is being sued. The standard utilized is that plaintiff must allege a short and plain statement of a claim showing that she is entitled to some relief. Consistent with this liberal approach, the plaintiff can plead alternatively and inconsistently, even within the same count. Fed.Rule 8(e)(2). Similarly, although the plaintiff must include a demand for relief, Fed.Rule 8(a)(3), the court is not bound by the demand in a contested case and can award whatever relief is appropriate.

Fed.Rule 54(c). The ad damnum clause limits recovery only in default situations. Finally, the rules require courts to construe the pleadings liberally so as to do substantial justice. Fed.Rule 8(f). A good illustration of the simplicity of federal pleading is the Official Forms produced by the rulemakers. See, e.g., Forms 5, 6, 8, and 11.

The only exception to the very liberal pleading requirements of the federal rules is in some very specific types of cases in which, by special rule, more detail is required. See Fed.Rule 9. For example, in fraud actions it is not enough to allege merely that the defendant committed a fraud. Rather, the pleader must allege the circumstances surrounding the fraud. The same is true in actions for defamation. The different treatment given to these actions undoubtedly reflects, in part, the fact that they are "disfavored" actions. Traditionally, the courts have scrutinized these types of actions rigorously because of their potential as tools of harassment. To discourage frivolous suits in these areas, a higher pleading threshold applies.

The reason for the general de-emphasis on factual revelation in the federal pleading rules was the desire of the rulemakers to eliminate some of the pleading-motion practice that occurs under the code system in which significant amounts of time and money are spent on technicalities prior to reaching the merits of the case. The burden of fact revelation is placed on the discovery process (see §§ 3–21—3–33, below), eliminating what often were definitional squabbles at the pleading stage. Of course, one necessary effect of liberalizing the pleading requirements is to lower the threshold for bringing an action in the federal courts. The notice-giving philosophy of the federal system makes an early dismissal on the pleadings almost impossible to obtain.

§ 3–5. The Reply

Under both code and federal procedure, pleadings beyond the complaint and answer are generally disfavored or forbidden. This development reflects the de-emphasis on pleadings in modern legal systems. In certain limited circumstances, the plaintiff may be allowed, or even required, to file a reply. For example, most pleading rules require the plaintiff to file a reply to counterclaims made by the defendant. However, a majority of courts do not permit a reply to affirmative defenses, treating them as automatically denied. When a reply is filed, the plaintiff is in a defensive posture, responding to the defendant's allegations, and the general rules governing responsive pleading apply. See § 3–6, below. No pleadings beyond the reply are permitted.

2. DEFENDANT

§ 3–6. The Answer

The defendant has several options as to how to respond to the plaintiff's complaint under both the state codes and the federal rules. As is discussed later, see § 3–8, below, the defendant can enter a plea in abatement either by motion or in the answer. The defendant also can enter a denial, can introduce an affirmative defense, and can seek independent relief from the plaintiff. Each of these last three options may be used alternatively or in combination. In addition, the defendant may admit the allegations in the complaint, either by specifically acknowledging their truth or, more commonly, by failing properly to deny them. All of these responses should be included in the defendant's responsive pleading—the answer.

There are five different types of denials that may be used. Each one places in issue the matter denied. The major problem in deciding which to utilize is that the denial must be truthful and cannot be misleading; the defendant only can place in issue those matters that actually are in dispute. A *general denial* puts in issue all matters set forth in the complaint, and thus typically cannot be utilized truthfully. Alternatively, the defendant can enter a *specific denial,* denominating those paragraphs that are in dispute. The failure to deny the other paragraphs results in their admission. See Fed.Rule 8(d). Similarly, a *qualified denial* may be used, denying only specific averments within a given paragraph. These three types of denials are the most common. Most judicial systems also allow a denial on the ground that the defendant has *insufficient knowledge to form a belief* as to the truth or falsity of a given allegation in the complaint. This form of denial must be used with caution. The issue must be one outside the defendant's knowledge and, further, one about which the defendant could not easily have informed himself. It is unclear exactly what burden is placed on the defendant to gain the requisite knowledge and the court will decide on a case-by-case basis whether that defense is legitimate. If the denial is found inappropriate, the matter which was so denied will be deemed admitted. The last form of denial that may be utilized is a *denial on information and belief*. This approach is used most often by corporate defendants who are being sued because of the activities of their employees. It is permitted because the information available to the corporation at the time of filing the answer may be only secondhand. This denial allows them to protect themselves should later information reveal the truth of some of the plaintiff's allegations.

In addition to pleading some form of denial, the defendant may include affirmative defenses in the answer. Affirmative defenses are descendants of the common law plea in confession and avoidance: the defendant admits the truth of plaintiff's allegation, but alleges new facts that require the dismissal of the action. Unlike common law practice, however, affirmative defenses may be used in conjunction with denials. The defendant in admitting the plaintiff's allegations does so only for purposes of the defense. Examples of affirmative defenses are statute of limitations, res judicata, assumption of the risk, and release. Any defense that seeks to avoid the plaintiff's allegations by introducing new facts, rather than attempting to destroy the allegations in the complaint may be deemed an affirmative defense. This definition is an important one to understand; the failure to include an affirmative defense in the answer usually will result in its waiver. The rationale for this rule is that because the defense introduces new facts, its omission from the pleadings fails to notify the plaintiff so that it would be unfair to allow its assertion at a later time. Although the courts sometimes will allow amendments to raise these defenses, see §§ 3–9—3–10, below, the ability to amend is a limited one. Thus, a good rule of thumb is: when in doubt as to whether a given defense is affirmative, plead it.

The final matter to consider including in the answer is a request for some affirmative or independent relief from the plaintiff. This is referred to either as a counterclaim or cross-complaint. The rules regarding when a defendant is permitted to seek affirmative relief in this manner are discussed elsewhere, see § 3–20, below. For pleading purposes, a defendant in this position is treated like a claimant and the same pleading requirements that govern the complaint control the assertion of a claim in the answer.

3.   ASSURING TRUTHFULNESS IN PLEADING

§ 3–7.   Signature and Verification Requirements

The two most common methods used to promote truthfulness in pleading and discourage the filing of frivolous claims and defenses are an attorney signature requirement and verification. In many jurisdictions, the attorney is required to sign the pleadings and that signature stands as a certification that the claim or defense is filed in good faith—that there are good grounds to support it and that it is not interposed for purposes of delay. Although these provisions stand as a reminder to attorneys of their obligations to the legal system, they have not been very effective as control devices because, among other things, judges have been reluctant to impose sanctions for violation of the signature requirements unless there is a finding of subjective bad faith—a most difficult element to prove.

Recognizing these enforcement problems, the federal rules were amended in 1983 to provide that the attorney signature is to be affixed only after "a reasonable inquiry" as to whether there are sufficient grounds in law and in fact to support the pleadings. Fed.Rule 11. Sanctions for noncompliance were made mandatory. These changes were designed to allow the court to apply objective criteria as to the attorneys' reasonable inquiry and to enlarge the use of the sanction power so as to deter marginal conduct. Considerable litigation involving Rule 11 occurred after its amendment and questions were raised concerning very basic features of the revised requirement, as well as whether the amended rule was achieving its purpose or was breeding a new form of satellite litigation. Thus, there was substantial pressure to revise the rule and 1993 amendments were made to try to respond to some of the criticism.

The revised rule continues to utilize an objective, rather than a subjective, bad faith standard for assessing whether the signer made a reasonable inquiry and concluded that the pleading was well-grounded in fact and law. See Business Guides, Inc. v. Chromatic Communications Enterprises, Inc. (S.Ct.1991). It also is expanded to cover all written motions and other papers filed in the litigation. Sanctions for violations are now discretionary, however, and a "safe harbor" provision is included by which parties desiring to request sanctions must wait at least 21 days after the paper has been filed and, if the alleged violation is cured in that period, no sanction motion can be filed. Fed.Rule 11(c)(1)(A). Whether the amended rule will achieve the proper balance between deterring frivolous filings and yet allowing attorneys to bring claims and defenses that they believe are meritorious but that may be less well grounded than others remains to be seen.

Verification requirements differ from the attorney certification prerequisites in that the pleader by verifying swears under oath as to the truth of all the allegations in the pleading. Thus, this requirement has practical utility only in situations in which facts are pleaded on which it would be useful to have the pleader attest to the truth thereof at the outset. Most judicial systems have abolished mandatory verification, except in certain special cases, such as in shareholder derivative suits, see Fed.Rule

23.1, or pleadings in attachment proceedings, see Ill.Smith–Hurd Ann. ch. 110, ¶¶ 4–104, 4–131. Some states retain an optional verification scheme—the plaintiff may in her discretion verify the complaint, but if she does, the defendant then must verify the answer. Cal.Civ.Proc.Code § 446. This prevents the defendant from using a general denial. Although the application of strict verification requirements has the potential of being a trap for the unwary, modern courts generally have refused to apply sanctions for technical violations of these rules when the interests of justice would not be served thereby. See Surowitz v. Hilton Hotels Corp. (S.Ct.1966).

4. CHALLENGES TO THE PLEADINGS

§ 3–8. Methods of Challenging the Pleadings

There are a wide range of challenges that may be made to the pleadings. Most commonly, challenges are made by the defendant who seeks to dismiss or delay the action on grounds unrelated to the merits. However, the plaintiff also may attempt to challenge the defendant's pleadings. The possibility of interposing an objection primarily to delay the time when a responsive pleading must be filed has resulted in these types of objections being referred to as dilatory pleas.

The types of challenges that may be made are the same in code pleading and federal rule jurisdictions. The major difference between the two systems is in form. Objections to the pleadings in code states are made either by a motion to quash or by general or special demurrer, whereas objections under the federal rules are made by a specifically denominated motion or they may be included in the responsive pleading.

In general, the kinds of challenges available can be divided into four categories. In the first category, the defendant may object to the court's power to entertain the action, i.e. objections to personal and subject-matter jurisdiction and venue, or to some defect in the parties. In the second category, the defendant's challenge is to the complaint itself. By general demurrer or a motion to dismiss under Federal Rule 12(b)(6), the defendant can argue that the plaintiff has failed to state a claim for relief or a cause of action. This challenge can be directed to the entire complaint or to only some counts in the complaint. It points only to defects on the face of the complaint: the plaintiff actually may possess a claim, he simply has not properly pleaded one. Thus, most often dismissals on this ground are with leave to amend and the demurrer or motion acts merely to search the record. Both of these types of challenges are directed toward claims for relief rather than defenses and consequently are utilized most frequently by defendants. However, when the defendant has included a claim for relief (a counterclaim) in the answer, the plaintiff may raise either challenge as well.

The third type of challenge that may be made also is based on pleading defects. The object is not to obtain a dismissal, but to cure alleged deficiencies in the pleadings. Either a plaintiff or a defendant may make a motion to strike specific paragraphs or sentences. Objections operating as the basis for a motion to strike may challenge matter that is redundant or immaterial or that which is sham or scandalous. The motion to strike acts to prune the pleadings and generally is disfavored, given the great de-emphasis on the pleadings in modern litigation. In addition to a motion to strike, the defendant can question any matter that is ambiguous, unintelligible or generally uncertain in the complaint by special demurrer or by a motion for a more definite statement. This challenge cannot be used merely as a fishing device and is only available to a party who is required to file a responsive pleading. Given the few situations in which the plaintiff is allowed to file a reply (see § 3–5, above), this objection is one made most typically by defendants. The general standard used by the courts in deciding whether to grant these motions is whether the defects are such that the defendant cannot respond adequately unless a more definite statement is made. If a responsive pleading could be made without any additional information, then the challenge will be overruled and the defendant must rely on discovery to flesh out or clarify the case further.

The fourth and final pleading challenge that occurs is when the parties seek to attack the substantive sufficiency of the allegations by making a motion for judgment on the pleadings. This motion differs from the motion to dismiss in that, as its title suggests, it cannot be made until the pleadings are closed, i.e., both the complaint and answer are filed. In essence, a request for a judgment on the pleadings challenges not only the pleading sufficiency of the opponent, but whether a substantive right to relief or a legally sufficient defense exists on the facts as presented in the pleadings. Thus, its use typically is limited to situations in which the facts as shown in the complaint and answer reveal an affirmative defense absolutely barring plaintiff's claim, such as the statute of limitations. Conversely, it may be used when the sole defense relied upon by defendant in the answer is insufficient as a matter of law, such as if a defendant were to plead the statute of frauds in a case in which the plaintiff alleged a written contract.

B. AMENDED AND SUPPLEMENTAL PLEADINGS

§ 3–9. General Standards and Practice

At common law the pleadings assumed a dominant and controlling role and the ability to amend was virtually nonexistent. No variance was tolerated between the pleadings and the proof at trial and a departure in the evidence from the issue as framed in the pleadings led to the dismissal of the suit.

Modern code and federal practice differs radically from this approach. Amendments to the pleadings are allowed quite liberally in an effort to decide cases on their merits, rather than on technicalities, and a variance between the pleadings and the proof is permissible. Amendments have been allowed at trial and even after judgment in an effort to render justice. Courts generally will exercise their discretion to refuse an amendment only if allowing it would cause undue prejudice to the opposing party. This may occur, for example, if an amendment is sought so late that evidence that might disprove the new allegations no longer is available.

An amendment to conform the pleadings to the proof that is introduced at trial also may be utilized. If evidence is presented at trial on an issue not raised in the pleadings and no objection is raised, the court may deem the pleadings amended by the implied consent of the opposing party. See Fed. Rule 15(b). The overriding concern in deciding whether to allow this type of amendment necessarily is the existence of knowing consent on the part of the opponent.

In addition to the ability to amend, a number of jurisdictions authorize the filing of supplemental pleadings, Fed.Rule 15(d). As distinguished from amended pleadings, they seek to present matters that actually have occurred since the original pleadings were filed; amendments present omitted matters that occurred prior to the time suit was filed. For example, a supplemental pleading might be used to add related claims that have newly arisen in a case involving a continuing nuisance. Their availability eases the burden on the pleader who otherwise would be forced to file an entirely new action to present the newly arising claims.

§ 3–10. Statutes of Limitation: Relation Back

The most difficult problem involving amendments arises when a proposed amendment seeks to add a new claim or party after the statute of limitations has run. This problem commonly is described in terms of whether the amendment will be allowed to relate back to the institution of the action. The problem is really one of notice: did the opposing party have notice within the statutory period that this new claim would be asserted? If not, the amendment should not be allowed to relate back.

The notice issue is handled somewhat differently depending on whether the amendment proposes to add a new claim between already existing parties or seeks to add new parties themselves. In the first situation, the amendment typically will be allowed if the new facts or theories being alleged are part of the same cause of action (code states) or arise out of the same transaction or occurrence (federal rules practice) that is presented in the original pleadings. This standard is designed to assure that the new claim bears a close relationship with the claims already in the action. Notice is presumed because of the relationship of the amendment to the original pleadings.

The addition of new parties does not allow the same presumption. Thus, under the federal rules not only must the amendment present a transactionally related claim, but also the court must be able to find that the new party received actual notice of the claim before the time for filing the claim lapsed and knew that, but for a mistake, he should have been a named party. Fed.Rule 15(c). Notice need not mean service of process, but must involve more than knowledge that the plaintiff was injured. The federal court can allow an amendment adding a new party to relate back if doing so would be permitted under state law, Fed.Rule 15(c)(1), or if the party received notice within the period authorized for service under the federal rules. See Fed.Rule 4(m).

Practice in code pleading states is somewhat more ambiguous. There is no separate test for amendments adding parties; the cause of action test governs all amendments. Typically, the presence of a new party means that there is a new cause of action because different rights and duties are at issue. Thus, party amendments are strictly limited.

In some states, such as California, John Doe complaints are allowed and an issue arises as to whether the substitution of a real party for the fictitious one can be accomplished through an amendment relating back to the filing of the complaint. The courts have interpreted cause of action in these circumstances to mean the same facts, which would appear to allow unlimited amendments to substitute actual persons for John Does. However, the court will look carefully at the complaint to make certain that the claim being asserted against the newly named party was clearly contemplated in the original complaint. Totally new claims against new parties cannot be accomplished by using the John Doe device, even though they arise out of the same facts. On the other hand, if the claim was clearly within the scope of the complaint, the amendment will be allowed even though there was no actual notice to those parties.

C. JOINDER OF PARTIES AND CLAIMS

1. PARTY JOINDER

§ 3–11. Parties Who Must Be Joined

Although generally the plaintiff decides where, when and whom to sue, the plaintiff is not given complete freedom. Rules denominating who are real parties in interest and who are necessary or indispensable parties to the action restrict plaintiff's options to a limited extent. See §§ 3–12—3–13, below.

The rules governing who must be joined serve several important functions. As the name suggests, real party in interest rules assure that the named plaintiff is the person who possesses the substantive right being sued upon. (Compare the rules regarding who has standing to sue in § 9–1, below.) If the suit is not brought by a real party in interest, it may be dismissed unless a proper plaintiff can be joined. In this way, the defendant is protected from potentially harassing and duplicative litigation. Historically, real party in interest rules provided a means of identifying the actual owner of a right when there had been an assignment or some other transfer in interest prior to the action. In modern times, the rule simply clarifies who is a proper party plaintiff. See, e.g., Fed.Rule 17(a).

In the federal courts the designation of the real party in interest traditionally denominated the person whose citizenship controls for purposes of diversity jurisdiction. This latter function of the rule posed some problems in cases in which it was alleged that a nonresident administrator was appointed or an assignment was made so as to create or destroy federal diversity jurisdiction. Thus, the Supreme Court struck down an assignment of interest solely for collection purposes that was accomplished so as to create diversity. Kramer v. Caribbean Mills, Inc. (S.Ct.1969). Further, as was discussed in § 2–3, above, Congress amended the diversity statute to provide that administrators and guardians are deemed to be citizens of the same state as the state of the decedents, infants or incompetents they represent. Thus, although the administrator remains the real party in interest and is the proper party to file suit, that fact does not affect the question whether diversity jurisdiction may be established.

The necessary and indispensable party rules compel party joinder in order to protect persons who might be harmed by a judgment entered in their absence or, conversely, to protect existing parties who might not be able to obtain complete relief without the presence of those absent persons. The focus is on the impact of the judgment if the absentees are not joined. The difference between a necessary and an indispensable party has posed some problems for the courts. See § 3–13, below. Nonetheless, the rules serve the important function of protecting existing parties, as well as absent persons, from piecemeal or harmful litigation. For a more complete exploration of the various rules surrounding mandatory party joinder, see J. Friedenthal, M. Kane & A. Miller, *Civil Procedure* §§ 6.3 and 6.5 (2d ed.1993).

§ 3–12. Real Parties in Interest and Capacity to Sue

Real party in interest rules should be distinguished from rules governing a party's capacity to sue or be sued. The former attempt to assure that the named plaintiff possesses the substantive right on which the suit is based. Capacity rules focus on whether a party is qualified to appear as a named party in an action. They are dependent upon the character of the parties, not the rights involved. Typically, rules denying legal capacity are designed to protect certain classes of persons who might not be able to adequately protect their own interests, or they derive from the regulation of certain organizations or legal relationships. Criteria such as age and mental ability often determine a person's capacity to sue. For example, a minor child who is harmed in an automobile accident has no capacity to sue, although she does possess a cause of action. Her guardian or parents will be deemed real parties in interest and, having capacity, may sue for her. In this way, the capacity rules allow the person in the best position to pursue the child's rights to do so. In contrast, certain organizations, such as non-resident corporations, may be deprived of capacity because they have not registered to do business in the state and no one else may sue in their behalf. Because capacity rules focus on the abilities of certain classes of persons, rather than the question whether they possess a claim for relief, they apply both to plaintiffs and defendants.

§ 3–13. Necessary and Indispensable Parties

The question whether a party is necessary or indispensable to a particular lawsuit turns largely on the degree or directness of the absentee's interest in the action. The principle supporting compulsory joinder is an equitable one—an attempt to assure that any judgment entered will do justice for all concerned. Necessary parties may be defined as persons who have an interest in the litigation and whose interest might *possibly* be affected by a judgment entered in their absence. Indispensable parties possess interests that would *inevitably* be affected by any decree in the suit. Any person who is found to be either necessary or indispensable should be joined.

In some cases, however, joinder may be impossible because the person may not be within the personal jurisdiction reach of the court. In the federal courts, joinder also may be prevented because the presence of the new party would destroy diversity of citizenship, the court's subject-matter jurisdiction. In either situation, the determination of whether the absentee is necessary or is indispensable then becomes crucial. If he is merely necessary, the suit may proceed in his absence. If he is indispensable, it must be dismissed. Because of the serious effects of a finding of indispensability, courts evaluating this question will look carefully to see whether the decree can be shaped in such a way to avoid inevitably affecting the absentee's interest or to grant some relief to the existing parties in his absence. If so, then the absentee will be deemed only necessary and the suit need not be dismissed.

In the federal system the rulemakers in 1966 abandoned the terminology and approach of deciding compulsory joinder questions in terms of who is a necessary or indispensable party. Rather than focusing on categories of parties, federal practice requires the court to consider specific pragmatic factors in order to balance the equities of the situation and reach a decision. The United States Supreme Court interpreted the federal joinder provision, Fed.Rule 19, in Provident Tradesmens Bank & Trust Co. v. Patterson (S.Ct.1968). The Court suggested the following approach to compulsory joinder questions.

Once it is determined that the absentee has an interest in the litigation that might practically be impaired by a decree in his absence or that might prevent the existing parties to the suit from obtaining complete relief, that person is a Rule 19(a) party and should be joined. If he cannot be, Rule 19(b) sets out four factors for the court to consider and balance in deciding whether to dismiss or to proceed without the absent party. First, it should consider

the plaintiff's interest in the forum and whether
another forum might accommodate better all those
interested.   Second, it should determine whether
the failure to dismiss will subject the defendant to
multiple litigation.   Third, the interest of the absent person should be examined carefully to see
whether it will be foreclosed as a practical matter
by the judgment or if there is some way of shaping
the relief or staying the execution of the judgment
in order to protect his interest.   Fourth, the court
should consider judicial economy and whether the
present action represents an efficient means of settling the underlying dispute.   Although the Supreme Court did not explain what weight to give
each of the four factors, it did suggest that the trial
courts should attempt to apply Rule 19(b) in such a
way as to avoid dismissal unless it is absolutely
required.   If the absentee seeks to intervene in the
action, none of these concerns need be addressed.

The equitable concerns behind the compulsory
party joinder rule are so important that the failure
to join an indispensable or Rule 19(b) party may be
raised by the court on its own motion, or it may be
raised on appeal even though the issue never was
addressed at trial.   Thus, some courts have characterized this defect in parties as constituting a lack
of subject-matter jurisdiction.   However, the defect
is not jurisdictional, but equitable, and it cannot be
invoked to collaterally attack an otherwise valid
judgment.   Further, when raised for the first time
on appeal, the court may take into account the
untimeliness of the objection when considering the

prejudice that will accrue if joinder is not ordered; delay in making the motion effectively may be grounds for denial.

§ 3–14. Parties Who May Be Joined

Various rules exist governing who may be joined by the plaintiff in a lawsuit, who may be added to the lawsuit by the defendant or who may enter a lawsuit of their own volition. The addition of parties to an ongoing action is restricted by rule requirements, as well as by jurisdiction restraints. The court must be able to assert personal jurisdiction over each of the parties in the suit and, in the federal courts, subject-matter jurisdiction must be established over each of the claims between the various parties. The rules authorizing party joinder do not alter or affect the court's jurisdictional powers. The following sections will explore the requirements imposed by the rules on party joinder. A more detailed treatment of permissive party joinder may be found in J. Friedenthal, M. Kane & A. Miller, *Civil Procedure* §§ 6.4 and 6.9–6.10 (2d ed.1993).

§ 3–15. Proper Parties

The term proper parties refers to those persons whom the plaintiff may join as parties to the action when it is commenced. The joinder of a proper party is totally permissive so that the failure to join an otherwise proper party will not result in the dismissal of the suit. Under most code systems, which follow equity practice, any person who has an interest in the subject matter of the suit or the relief may be joined in the action. Unfortunately, most courts under the early codes ruled that any person joined must have an interest in all the relief being sought. Under this restrictive interpretation, a husband and wife could not join as plaintiffs in a suit arising out of a car accident if they each were asserting personal injury claims because neither plaintiff would have a legal interest in the personal injury recovery of the other. Other state courts interpret this requirement liberally and literally, encouraging joinder.

Under modern joinder practice, as exemplified by the federal rules, the joinder of proper parties is determined by a standard designed to promote judicial economy and prevent the action from becoming unwieldy or cluttered with unrelated parties and claims. If the claims for relief by or against the persons sought to be joined arise out of the same transaction or occurrence or series thereof and if the joined parties share *any* common question of law or fact, then joinder is proper. See Fed.Rule 20. The issue of what constitutes a transaction is within the court's discretion and frequently depends upon the number and centrality of the common questions that exist. The greater the overlap in evidence, the more efficiency that will be gained by allowing joinder. In the case of defendant joinder, the courts also may be inclined to construe transaction broadly because to disallow joinder may produce inconsistent verdicts and ultimately leave the plaintiff remediless.

§ 3–16. Impleaded Parties (Third–Party Defendants)

In order to provide defending parties an opportunity to more fully protect themselves, most procedural systems provide some mechanism by which the defendant can bring in (implead) a third-party defendant. See Fed.Rule 14. The two requirements for impleader are that the person is not already a party to the action and that the person "is or may be liable" to the defendant if the defendant is found liable to the original plaintiff. Thus, the most common theories for impleader are that the third-party defendant has a duty to indemnify the defendant or to contribute to the payment of plaintiff's damages. It is irrelevant that the impleaded party is directly liable to the plaintiff; he must have some legal liability towards the defendant. In the absence of impleader, the defendant would have to wait to file suit until after losing the main action. Impleader avoids this time lag between judgments and, because all the issues are decided in one action, it increases the likelihood of consistent results.

Once a third-party defendant has been joined to the action, he is allowed to assert not only defenses to the impleader claim, but also defenses to the main action that the original defendant may have omitted. Personal defenses, such as a lack of personal jurisdiction, may not be asserted on behalf of the original defendant. By allowing the third-party defendant to assert defenses to the main action, he can protect himself from liability should the original defendant be lax in this regard. This also protects the third-party defendant from potential collusion between the original plaintiff and defendant (the third-party plaintiff). Subject to jurisdictional limitations (see § 2–5, above), the third-party defendant also may assert claims against any of the parties to the action. Conversely, the other parties to the suit can assert additional claims directly against the impleaded defendant if they meet the jurisdictional requirements. This free assertion of claims between the parties is permitted under the rules in order to decide the entire dispute in a single action, thereby promoting judicial economy.

The decision whether to permit the impleader claim, as well as the filing of any additional claims is left to the court's discretion. The court will determine whether the joinder of this additional party or of the other claims will unduly complicate the action, improperly delay the determination of the main claim to the detriment of the original plaintiff, or confuse the jury. If so, joinder may be refused even though the claims fall within the rule's requirements.

§ 3–17. Other Additional Parties

The assertion of a proper counterclaim or cross-claim between the existing parties to an action, see § 3–20, below, may prompt the addition of another party whose presence would further the adjudication of that claim. See Fed.Rule 13(h). In some instances the party may be deemed indispensable to an adjudication of the new claim so that joinder will be ordered or the claim will be dismissed, see § 3–

13, above. Other parties who have lesser interests also may be joined, as long as they meet the standard of proper parties, see § 3–15, above. When testing the propriety of their joinder, the court will look at the relationship or interest of the additional parties to the counterclaim or cross-claim involved, rather than their relationship to the main action.

§ 3–18. Intervenors

An intervenor is a person who is not already a party to an ongoing action but who seeks to be made a party, typically because she shares some interest in the litigation and is concerned that in her absence that interest will not be adequately protected. The decision whether to allow intervention is based on a balancing of the needs or interests of the intervenor against the possible burdens on the existing parties if intervention is permitted. The court will consider whether the intervenor's claim shares common issues with the existing parties; the more the intervenor is attempting to inject new issues, the greater the potential prejudice and delay to the original action. An intervenor need not argue that she will be prejudiced because she will be bound by the judgment if not joined. Intervention is permissible if she can show that her interest will be impaired as a practical matter. The timeliness of a motion to intervene also is important because the greater the delay by the intervenor, the greater the likelihood of prejudice to the existing parties.

In the federal courts a distinction is drawn between intervention as of right, Fed.Rule 24(a), and permissive intervention, Fed.Rule 24(b). Under the former provision, if the intervenor demonstrates an interest in the action that might be impaired if intervention is not allowed, and the opposing parties do not show that that interest is already adequately represented, intervention will be allowed. In general, courts have interpreted these requirements liberally to accommodate multiparty litigation that will resolve finally a particular controversy. Thus, an intervenor has been found to have a sufficient interest so as to fall within Rule 24(a) even though the interest is not an economic one—such as parents seeking to intervene in a suit challenging the way in which a school board administers the schools. And, although inadequate representation may be found when there are clearly conflicting interests between the intervenor and the existing parties, it also may be established when the intervenor's claim is sufficiently different from those already in the action that no one there is likely to vigorously pursue it. The courts obviously have considerable leeway in deciding what constitutes a sufficient interest or whether the interest is already protected, but their discretion is not boundless. Once the standard is met, intervention cannot be denied simply because it would delay the action or prejudice the existing parties. If the rule's requirements are satisfied, intervention must be granted as long as the presence of the intervenor does not destroy diversity jurisdiction. The 1990 supplemental jurisdiction statute specifically excludes intervenors from supplemental jurisdiction, 28 U.S.C.A. § 1367(b), even though prior to its enactment courts routinely held intervenors of right to be within their ancillary jurisdiction. See § 2–5, above.

The premise for permissive intervention is merely that common questions exist and the court is given complete discretion to deny intervention despite a finding that the rule requirements are met. Although timeliness may be taken into account for intervention under both Fed.Rule 24(a) and Fed. Rule 24(b), the courts are much more inclined to grant a late motion to intervene as of right than one for permissive intervention. The difference between permissive intervention and intervention as of right also is important in the federal courts in other contexts. For example, different rules are applied to determine the appealability of orders denying intervention as of right and permissive intervention. The former may be appealed immediately; the latter are appealable only if the appellate court finds that the trial judge abused his discretion in denying intervention.

2. CLAIM JOINDER

§ 3–19. Claim Joinder—In General

The ability to join several claims in one suit depends upon rules authorizing joinder and whether the claims are within the court's jurisdictional power. This latter prerequisite is important primarily in the federal courts as they have only limited subject-matter jurisdiction and the application of a joinder rule cannot operate to extend their power. In the state courts the primary concern is whether joinder is authorized under the procedural rules governing the judicial system where suit is brought.

There are two types of rules governing claim joinder that should be distinguished. The first authorizes defending parties to introduce certain claims against opposing or co-parties, such as counterclaims and cross-claims. These are discussed in the next section. The second and more general provisions deal with whether a party with authorization to interject some claims into the action, may join with those claims additional claims against the same party. Most commonly, these rules are invoked by a plaintiff seeking to join several claims against a defendant, but they also may be used by defendants desiring to assert multiple counterclaims or cross-claims. For simplicity's sake, the remainder of this section will speak of these latter rules as plaintiff claim joinder rules, but it should not be forgotten that they also control the joinder possibilities of any party seeking to assert multiple claims against an opponent.

The rules governing joinder of claims by the plaintiff fall into three categories. The first is derived from the Field Code and lists a series of categories, permitting the plaintiff to join any claims that fall into a single category. See, e.g., Cal.Civ.Proc.Code § 427. In all but one category, claims are joined by subject matter (e.g., injury to the person, injury to property, contracts). In the remaining category, joinder is permitted because of a unity of occurrence—claims "arising out of the same transaction or transactions connected with the same subject of the action." Further restrictions in some code pleading systems that the joined claims must affect all the parties to a dispute and must present consistent, not alternative, theories of recovery prevent joinder from being too broad. The misjoinder of claims may be challenged by demurrer and the suit dismissed until properly pleaded.

The second category of claim joinder rule places no limitations on the plaintiff. See, e.g., Fed.Rule 18(a). Plaintiff is permitted to join as many claims, related or unrelated, as she may have against the defendant. Concerns about potential prejudice due to jury confusion or the convenience of trying all the claims in one suit are decided at the trial stage, when the court may order a severance of one or more of the claims for a separate trial. Misjoinder under these rules is impossible at the pleading stage.

The third type of joinder provision allows the plaintiff the same freedom to join unrelated claims, but includes a compulsory joinder provision, requiring the joinder of all claims arising out of the same transaction or occurrence. See, e.g., Mich.Gen. Ct.R. 203. In this way judicial economy is assured and the defendant is protected against a series of potentially harassing suits. Notably, although both of the other approaches speak only of permissive joinder, the plaintiff's options under any system may be restricted by the judicial doctrines of res judicata and collateral estoppel, see §§ 6–5—6–14, below. The potential application of those doctrines to prevent a second or third action may create some compulsion on the plaintiff to join all related claims in one action. The inclusion of a compulsory joinder provision in the rule itself clarifies the hazards of failing to join those claims and also simplifies the second court's inquiry as to whether a subsequent action should be barred.

§ 3–20. Defendant Joinder: Counterclaims and Cross–Claims

The constraints placed upon the defendant's freedom to assert and to join claims stem both from rule and jurisdictional limitations. Thus, even though the joinder of defendant's claims may be permissible under the rules, each new claim also must have some jurisdictional basis. Before considering the rule requirements, a few terminological remarks are necessary. In some states all claims asserted by a defendant are denominated "cross-complaints." Other states, as well as the federal courts, distinguish between claims asserted against opposing parties ("counterclaims") and claims between co-parties ("cross-claims"). Different limitations are placed on the defendant in each of these two situations. Thus, it is important to be careful to distinguish between cross-complaints and cross-claims as the latter is a term of art referring only to a very specific situation.

There are three questions to address when considering the propriety of defendant claim joinder. The first is what claims the defendant has the power to assert against the other parties to the action. The second question is whether the defendant can join additional claims to those specifically authorized under the rules. The third is whether the defendant can join additional parties against whom he wishes to assert a claim. It is the first question that will be addressed in this section. The defendant's ability to join additional claims is governed by the same rules and principles applicable to plaintiff claim joinder, see § 3–19, above. The addition of parties to the action is discussed in §§ 3–16—3–17, above.

All judicial systems permit the defending party, as a matter of rule practice, to assert any claims he may have against the opposing party, typically the plaintiff. The modern day counterclaim traces its roots to the historic practice of recoupment and set-off. Recoupment allowed the defendant to reduce plaintiff's recovery by proving a transactionally related claim. Set-off permitted the defendant to assert unrelated, liquidated claims against the plaintiff. In either case, no affirmative relief beyond the plaintiff's claim was allowed and the defendant waived the right to claim any excess in a subsequent action.

Modern systems typically allow a defending party to assert any claims he has against his opponent, see, e.g., Fed.Rule 13. Additionally, most systems distinguish between counterclaims that are related to the opposing party's claim and those that are not. The defendant is required to assert any transactionally related claims, e.g., Fed.Rule 13(a), and is permitted to assert any others, e.g., Fed.Rule 13(b). This distinction between compulsory and permissive counterclaims is important because the failure to interpose a compulsory counterclaim will prevent the defendant from raising that claim in a separate action as a result of notions of waiver or estoppel.

The general standard determining whether a counterclaim is compulsory is whether the claim arises out of the same transaction or occurrence as the main action. This test typically will be met if there is a logical relationship between the claims, such as if they arise out of the same event, or if some of the same evidence must be used to prove both claims. There are a few exceptions to the compulsory counterclaim rules that act to protect the defendant from being under too great a burden. Thus, the defendant must assert only those transactionally related claims that are mature when the original complaint was served, that are not already the subject of pending litigation, and that do not require the presence of other parties over whom the court may not have jurisdiction. See Fed.Rule 13(a). Other rule provisions allow amendments prior to judgment to include omitted or newly discovered counterclaims. See Fed.Rules 13(e), (f). Additional exceptions have been created by the courts in order to protect further the defendant. For example, a defendant who has two separate actions pending against him and whose counterclaim is transactionally related to both, may choose in which action to assert the counterclaim and need not file it in the first proceeding that was brought. Of course, a defendant who wishes to assert any of these excepted counterclaims may do so.

Although a few states provide for the unrestricted assertion of cross-claims, see, e.g., N.Y.C.P.L.R. 3019(b), the ability of a defendant to assert claims against co-defendants typically is more limited than the ability to claim against an opposing party. In general, only cross-claims that are transactionally related to the main action are permitted under the rules. See Fed.Rule 13(g). Once a party has filed a proper cross-claim, however, she may join any additional claims she has against that party, even if they are unrelated. This is because the power to join claims is governed by the general claim joinder rules which typically are open-ended (see § 3–19, above), not the cross-claim provisions.

The rationale for restricting a party's initial right to cross-claim to transactionally related claims reflects a concern that the litigation of claims not directly involving the plaintiff may delay plaintiff's action and, to the extent it complicates the litigation, may prejudice the original suit. In contrast to the broader authority for counterclaims, the cross-claim limitation recognizes that complete justice between the plaintiff and the defendants can be accomplished without the adjudication of any cross-claims, whereas complete justice may not be achieved without adjudicating counterclaims. Thus, cross-claims are always permissive; the defendant may assert a claim against a co-defendant in a totally separate action without any risk of waiver or estoppel.

Although proper cross-claims, like compulsory counterclaims, are governed by a transaction test, there is greater disagreement among the courts as to what constitutes the same transaction for cross-claim purposes. This reflects the fact that cross-claims bring into play two conflicting concerns. Some courts emphasize the desire to decide an entire dispute in one action, even though it involves a series of claims between different parties. They define the transaction very broadly. A good example of this broad joinder philosophy is a dispute arising out of a large construction project, involving claims of breach of contract between the contractors, subcontractors, architects, and the sureties. Other courts are concerned about unnecessarily complicating and delaying the plaintiff's action and, in order to prevent that from happening, interpret transaction narrowly to include only claims in which the rights of the plaintiff are implicated in some way.

D. DISCOVERY

1. IN GENERAL

§ 3–21. General Principles Governing

The discovery phase of litigation serves several important purposes: it can be used to preserve evidence of witnesses who may not be available at the time of the trial; to reveal facts; to aid in formulating the issues; and to freeze testimony so as to prevent perjury. Discovery may serve to prepare a case for summary judgment as the parties discover that the only issues in contention are those of law. It also may promote settlements insofar as parties are able by careful inquiry to test the strength of their opponent's case. Even if it does not result in obviating the need for a trial, if properly utilized, discovery should aid in producing a crystallized trial. With full revelation of facts between the parties, the trial becomes less of a "game of wits" and more of a probing into the actual truth of certain facts. This results in a systems savings, as well as a fairer or more just trial. Thus, it is not surprising that the federal courts and most of the states have provided for very liberal discovery. Indeed, at present, there are only a few limitations on the number or types of discovery devices that may be utilized in a single case.

The effectiveness of any discovery system depends in great measure on whether it can operate extrajudicially. Otherwise, the amount of time saved at trial is lost in litigation over discovery orders. In recognition of this fact, under the federal discovery rules, as well as in several states, the only time the parties appear before the court during discovery is when some problem or disagreement arises concerning the valid scope of an inquiry.

The provision of broad discovery is tied to the move away from special or rigid pleading rules. It represents a shift in the time at which a party must be able to prove his case. Notice pleading coupled with liberal discovery allows the parties to build their cases up to the point of trial, or at least summary judgment. Systems maintaining more rigid pleading rules limit discovery and typically permit it only with tight court supervision. The parties are required to know more and be able to show more about their case at the time suit is filed or they will not be allowed into court. Obviously these two approaches represent very different philosophies and strong arguments are made as to which is the better approach. What is important to be aware of is how and why discovery operates as it does.

The scope of discovery provided in the rules of most judicial systems illustrates the modern philosophy toward full disclosure. Generally, a party may seek any information that is relevant to the subject matter of the action, as long as it is not privileged. (See the exception for attorney work-product information in § 3–31, below.) The information need not be admissible at trial under the rules of evidence; it only must be reasonably calculated to lead to admissible evidence. The limitation for privileged matters refers to information that is transmitted between individuals in certain relationships, such as doctor-patient and lawyer-client. The law regards encouraging the confidence of persons in those relationships as more important than discovering what has transpired between them. The law of privileges is part of the Rules of Evidence and thus outside the scope of this volume. What is important here is merely to note how few restrictions exist on the scope of what may be discovered.

The discussion that follows will describe the various types of discovery devices available, using the federal system as the model. The federal procedures have been adopted in whole or in part in most states. However, the reader should be careful to check the specific rules of the jurisdiction in which suit is brought, as the amount of freedom in this area may vary somewhat from forum to forum. For a more complete discussion, see J. Friedenthal, M. Kane & A. Miller, *Civil Procedure* Ch. 7 (2d ed.1993).

§ 3–22. Mandatory Disclosure

In response to various criticisms of the existing federal discovery regime (see § 3–34, below), Federal Rule 26(a) was amended in 1993 to provide for the mandatory disclosure of certain information at the outset of the case to be later supplemented by further discovery. Fed.Rule 26(a)(5). This change was very controversial and opposed by most of the practicing bar and districts were allowed to opt out of this mandatory disclosure regime by local rule, which many have done. The main purpose of the amendments was to accelerate basic information exchanges between the parties, eliminating the paperwork otherwise involved in requesting the information.

To accomplish this, the rule requires three waves of disclosures. First, each party must provide its opponents with the names of individuals likely to have information relevant to facts alleged with particularity in the pleadings, as well as information regarding (or copies of) all relevant documents, data compilations and tangible things; a computation of the damages being sought by the disclosing party; and any insurance agreements indicating that an insurer will satisfy all or part of the judgment. Fed.Rule 26(a)(1). Second, parties must disclose information regarding any experts they may use at trial. Fed.Rule 26(a)(2). Third, shortly before trial, the parties must disclose information regarding any evidence that may be used at trial, such as names of witnesses and documentary or exhibit evidence intended to be used. Fed.Rule 26(a)(3). Whether this mandatory disclosure approach will accomplish its purposes and serve as a model for state courts or will create additional problems remains to be seen.

2. DISCOVERY DEVICES: THE MECHANICS AND TACTICS

§ 3–23. Depositions

Depositions are probably the most useful and most costly of discovery devices. They can be taken of a party or a witness. A deposition acts as a sort of minitrial. The person deposed (deponent) appears before a court officer and gives sworn testimony in response to questions by the attorneys from both sides of the case. The scope of the examination is not limited by the rules of evidence; the attorneys may inquire of anything relevant, as long as it is not privileged. Examination and cross-examination occurs with the opportunity to pursue new lines of inquiry as new facts are revealed and to test the deponent as a witness, not only as to the probable substance of the testimony, but also as to demeanor, quickness, confidence, etc. The testimony is transcribed, signed and sworn to.

Although depositions may be taken anytime after an action is commenced, most rules provide that the plaintiff cannot begin a deposition until some time after the defendant is served with process, usually twenty to thirty days. This allows the defendant to obtain a lawyer and ready the case so as to be prepared at the deposition. The one exception to this restriction is special provisions authorizing a deposition to be taken even before suit is filed. See, e.g., Fed.Rule 27. This procedure is available to perpetuate the testimony of persons who most likely will not be available at trial. It only can be invoked when the requesting party states why the action has not been or cannot be filed first.

The adversarial nature of the deposition permits its use at trial for a variety of purposes. It can be used to impeach a witness whose trial testimony varies from that of the deposition. It can be used for witnesses who are dead or outside the court's subpoena power at the time of trial. In the federal system, depositions can be introduced for witnesses more than 100 miles from the place of trial, see Fed.Rule 32(a)(3)(B). This willingness to allow "paper witnesses" because of inconvenience alone illustrates the strength of the deposition.

In many ways, the major drawback to depositions is their cost. Attorneys' fees for both sides, witness' fees, stenographers' fees and transcription costs can be extremely expensive, if not prohibitive. Further, although a party may be deposed wherever the suit is lodged, a nonparty can be commanded to appear there only if she is within the subpoena power of the court. See Fed.Rule 45(c)(3)(A). If a deposition is desired of a distant witness, the parties and their attorneys typically must travel to the witness, adding travel and subsistence costs to this already expensive procedure.

§ 3–24. Depositions Upon Written Questions

The major difference between depositions and depositions upon written questions is that the latter are scripted in advance. The scope of the examination in terms of who may be deposed and what information may be sought remains the same. Similarly, depositions upon written questions are governed by the same rules as oral depositions regarding their use at trial.

The side requesting this procedure sends a proposed list of questions to the opposing counsel, who in turn submits a series of cross-examination questions. Redirect and recross questions also may be exchanged. The deponent then appears before the court reporter and responds to this set of prepared questions, with all answers being transcribed, signed, and sworn to.

The chief advantage of this procedure is that it is less costly than a deposition, particularly when dealing with a distant witness. Because the examination is limited to questions submitted in advance, none of the attorneys need be present and, by definition, the procedure takes place wherever the deponent is located. Further, since the testimony is delayed until questions are exchanged, there is no fear of the witness being unprepared, and the procedure can be used by either party immediately after commencement of the action. However, the loss in spontaneity and flexibility in regard to what questions are asked suggests that it never should be used when deposing a hostile or key witness or when the subject under examination is very complicated. Not surprisingly, this device is not often utilized.

§ 3–25. Interrogatories

Interrogatories consist of a series of written questions to which written answers are prepared and signed under oath. They differ from depositions on written questions in that they may be directed only to parties, not witnesses, and the answers may be composed by the party and his attorney. Although technically the scope of proper inquiry is the same—relevant, but not privileged, information— the requestor is not limited to things within the respondent's personal knowledge. Facts may be solicited that require the party to search his records in order to answer. The responding party has no duty, however, to investigate into matters outside his direct control. Thus, interrogatories are most useful to discover organizational knowledge, which requires searching corporate records. They are the least expensive means of obtaining information; no burden or cost, except phrasing the questions, typically is placed on the requesting party. Although traditionally interrogatories were not limited as to the number that could be served, charges that they were subject to abuse and had become too burdensome have resulted in several judicial systems placing some restrictions on their use. For example, in 1993 the federal rules were amended to provide that a party may not serve more than 25 interrogatories, including all discrete subparts, on an adverse party except with leave of court or by written stipulation. Fed.Rule 33(a).

Interrogatories usually are not used as evidence at trial. Their admissibility depends on the rules of evidence in the trial court and this means, because of the hearsay and best evidence rules, that they ordinarily will be excluded. Thus, the primary use of interrogatories is as a start-up device. Based on the facts revealed in the answers to the interrogatories, the attorney better can determine what issues are presented and how to frame a deposition.

As noted earlier, interrogatories can be terribly burdensome and subject to considerable abuse. This is one reason why their exchange is limited to parties. In an effort to curtail some of these abuses in the business context, when response to interrogatories may require an investigation of business records, the federal rules and several states have provisions designed to allow the responding party to shift some of the burden onto the requesting party. Under these provisions a corporation can designate the records in which the answer to the interrogatories can be found and the requesting party then must search out the answer, see Fed.Rule 33(d). The respondent cannot use this protection to hide information, however, and must designate with some specificity what documents or files contain the information sought so that the party seeking discovery should be able to find it.

§ 3–26. Discovery of Documents and Things

Document discovery refers to the means by which parties can obtain access to documents and other items not in their possession. The requesting party seeks to inspect files or examine premises or other things in order to arrive at his own conclusions regarding the facts, rather than to propound interrogatories requiring the opponents to prepare answers after reviewing their own records. The party seeking discovery may make copies of those documents of interest, take photographs, or make whatever record is appropriate.

Modern discovery rules generally provide for document discovery between the parties as soon as the action is commenced. No court order is needed. The requesting party simply asks the opponent for access to the documents or things that she wishes to investigate. Any document that is relevant, not privileged, and within the possession or control of a party may be discovered. See Fed.Rule 34.

One of the main problems involved in obtaining discovery relating to property is determining when items are within the control of a party. Control does not mean legal control. If a party is in a position to influence the person or organization possessing the documents, the party will be deemed to control them. In the one case to reach the United States Supreme Court on this issue, Societe Internationale v. Rogers (S.Ct.1958), the Court ruled that the defendant would have to deliver documents to the plaintiff even though under Swiss law the revelation of those documents could result in a criminal penalty! The party had the ability to influence the Swiss government to change the law or to create an exception to it and thus had control over the documents.

Although the specific discovery rules relating to documents and things generally authorize discovery only from parties, nonparties also may be subject to document discovery under the subpoena power of the court. See Fed.Rule 45(a)(1)(C). Court control over this type of discovery from witnesses assures that it will not be too burdensome or intrusive—a charge often made regarding party discovery. Further, in the case of nonparties, the court may order production only on specified conditions designed to alleviate the hardship, such as reasonably compensating the answering party. See Fed.Rule 45(c)(3)(B)(iii).

§ 3–27. Physical and Mental Examinations

The one discovery device that remains under the complete control of the court is a request for the physical or mental examination of parties. This discovery device has survived constitutional attack and challenges that it violates the doctor-patient privilege, Sibbach v. Wilson & Co. (S.Ct.1941). However, its use is strictly limited to parties or persons under the custody or legal control of parties and to situations in which the need for information outweighs the right to privacy of the person being examined.

A court will order a physical or mental exam only upon a showing that the party's health is an actual issue in controversy in the case and that there is "good cause" for granting the request. Good cause under these circumstances means more than relevance. The requesting party must show why the information is necessary and that it cannot be obtained otherwise. There must be some basis for believing that the party is suffering from some relevant physical or mental disability. Further, although it now is settled that this discovery device may be utilized against both plaintiffs and defendants, the court may be more stringent in applying the "good cause" requirement when defendants are being examined. This distinction reflects an awareness that typically it is the plaintiff who shapes the controversy and thus easily could place the defendant's health in controversy. Despite these concerns, it is fair to say that in personal injury litigation today requests for physical and mental examinations are granted rather routinely. It is only in other litigation areas that these requests pose difficulties.

In recognition of the intrusion a court-ordered examination may represent, the rules provide some reciprocal privileges to the examinee. Upon request, the person examined must be given a copy of the doctor's report. This opportunity contrasts sharply with the generally more limited access allowed to expert witnesses, see § 3–32, below. However, if such a request is made, the opposing party then may obtain a copy of any similar reports by doctors retained by the examinee. By making the initial request, the examinee has waived the doctor-patient privilege.

§ 3–28. Admissions

Admissions are a discovery device designed to frame the issues or facts actually in controversy. An admission obtained during discovery will establish conclusively that issue at trial, unless the court allows its later amendment or withdrawal—a very uncommon practice. It will not control in any other lawsuit. Admissions are limited to parties and essentially operate by means of an exchange of papers between the parties. A party may request an admission on either an issue of law or fact concerning all matters relevant, but not privileged, and within the knowledge of the opposing party. The responding party can remain silent, in which case the issue will be deemed admitted; specifically admit or deny each request; object on the ground some requests concern irrelevant or privileged matter; or refuse to answer, stating in detail why he cannot deny or admit as requested.

It is this last option that has posed the greatest difficulty for the courts. What are sufficient grounds for refusing to answer? Two problems surface immediately. First, when is some matter outside the knowledge of the party so that no answer can be made? The respondent clearly need not conduct a detailed search for information in order to answer because that would place the party in the position of proving the other side's case. Nonetheless, some inquiry must be made. Second, can a party refuse to answer on the ground that the issue concerned is the essential issue in dispute and to answer would be to concede the case? Some state courts prohibit admissions on basic issues. Under the federal rules, a party cannot object to an admission on the ground that it involves a core issue in the case. See Fed.Rule 36(a). However, a party may in good conscience deny such a requested admission thereby placing the matter "at issue" for trial. In this way, at the least, the main issues for trial are framed.

§ 3–29. Objections to Discovery Requests

With the exception of requests for physical or mental examinations, discovery proceeds without court intervention unless some dispute arises. A party objecting to an inquiry made during the course of any of the discovery procedures described in the preceding sections may pursue one of two routes. The first is to answer all non-objectionable questions, registering an objection to those he refuses to answer. The party seeking discovery then can move for a court order compelling a response, at which time the examinee can explain the basis for the objections. Under this alternative the need for court intervention never may materialize, however, as the requesting party, after reviewing the responses that the party is willing to make, may decide that it is not necessary to pursue the unanswered questions. The other alternative is for the examinee to move for a protective order to allow him to avoid responding.

If the court orders a response to be made and the requesting party continues to refuse, sanctions may be imposed, see § 3–30, below. However, if the court upholds the objection, it may enter a wide range of protective orders, ranging from forbidding inquiry into certain matters, to allowing discovery but only under certain circumstances (e.g., a deposition placed under seal and allowed to be opened only by court order). A good listing of the types of protective orders available to the court can be found in Fed.Rule 26(c).

The question of how to object to a particular discovery request raises another important problem—how to obtain immediate appellate review of court orders requiring or limiting discovery. In most judicial systems appeals are permissible only after a judgment on the merits has been reached. See §§ 7–1—7–5, below. Interlocutory orders, such as discovery orders, must await the final judgment before being appealed. In many cases this will mean that the order is never reviewed by an appellate court because it will be most difficult to demonstrate that the discovery order, even if erroneous, was so prejudicial to the ultimate result as to merit a reversal. (Any error the trial court made in its order will be deemed harmless error, not subject to reversal.) There are only two means available to an attorney to obtain immediate review under these circumstances. The first is to petition for the extraordinary writ of mandamus. See § 7–5, below. Mandamus provides only very limited relief, however, because it is restricted to situations in which some gross miscarriage of justice or abuse of discretion occurred in the trial court. For example, mandamus was granted to review an order requiring the defendants to submit to nine physical examinations; the challenge raised the constitutional rights of the defendants. Schlagenhauf v. Holder (S.Ct.1964).

The second means of obtaining review is to refuse to obey the court order, be adjudged in contempt, and appeal from the final contempt judgment challenging the bases on which it was entered. This process is risky, however. No immediate appeal will be allowed if civil, rather than criminal, contempt is found. On the other hand, if criminal, rather than civil, contempt is involved, the scope of appellate review in some courts is so narrow that the court will not consider the objection to the underlying order which resulted in contempt. Further, in either case, if the appellate court upholds the lower court's discovery order, the contempt penalty will remain in effect. Thus, in most situations the trial court's discovery orders are final and binding.

§ 3–30. Protective Orders and Sanctions: Controlling Abuses

The potential for the discovery process to be abused is apparent—continual requests for information that is not essential, but fits within the broad notion of relevance, can be made to harass the opposing side, and obdurate refusals to respond to legitimate requests requiring court intrusion can be costly, as well as result in delay. Modern discovery provisions thus include several tools by which the courts are encouraged to protect against abuse and ensure that discovery is used for its legitimate purposes.

A common device that is used is the protective order, allowing the court to protect a person from harassment or unduly burdensome requests. Fed. Rule 26(c). Using this power, the court may eliminate discovery or limit it to only what is necessary. It also may control the time and place of discovery so as to protect parties from extremely inconvenient discovery demands. The federal courts are particularly encouraged to identify and discourage discovery abuse through provisions authorizing them to adopt local rules imposing limits on the number and length of discovery devices, as well as to issue orders on their own initiative to limit discovery that is too cumulative or that might be obtained in a less burdensome or expensive fashion. Fed.Rule 26(b)(2).

Along similar lines, the federal rules include a signature requirement for all discovery documents; the signature constitutes a certificate by the attorney that the request or response is not being made for an improper purpose and is not unreasonable. Sanctions, including attorney fees, are authorized for any violations. Fed.Rule 26(g). In this way, attorneys are encouraged to consider seriously the legitimacy of each discovery request and response.

In addition to these protective devices, every set of discovery rules contains a general provision for sanctions in the event court intervention is invoked to force a party to cooperate with a legitimate inquiry. See, e.g., Fed.Rule 37. Most commonly, the court is permitted to assess expenses. A party who forced an adjournment of a deposition, or who fails to appear for a properly noticed deposition or to answer or respond to an otherwise proper discovery request may be required to pay any expenses incurred by the opponent because of those tactics. In cases of wilful disobedience, the court may dismiss the case or enter a default judgment. Similarly, it may deem established all matters about which the party refused to respond or strike those matters from the pleadings. Finally, when the court has ordered a party to respond to certain inquiries and he has refused to do so, a contempt judgment may be entered, including a possible jail sentence and fine. The possibility of sanctions acts as a deterrent to attorneys who otherwise might be reluctant to cooperate fully in discovery. In general, courts have used their sanctioning power carefully, reserving the harshest sanctions for cases revealing flagrant abuses. The trial judge's decision to impose sanctions is also almost always unassailable because appellate courts will overturn it only if an abuse of discretion is found.

3. SPECIFIC PROBLEMS

§ 3–31. Attorney Work–Product

One of the serious problems that has faced courts having liberal discovery rules is how to prevent legal parasitism, by which one side in the litigation lessens its own investment and preparation by allowing the opponent to fully prepare the case and then discovering that attorney's work-product. To allow this kind of occurrence would destroy the adversary nature of the proceeding and debilitate the quality of the lawyering in the courts because it would inhibit maximum trial preparation.

Generally, attorney-client privilege rules protect only direct communications between the attorney and the client. They do not protect information from witnesses, investigative reports, internal memoranda, etc. Thus, the United States Supreme Court developed the work-product rule for the federal courts. It totally exempts from discovery the mental impressions, conclusions, opinions or legal theories of the opposing attorney. Further, the attorney's other work-product is not discoverable unless the person requesting access shows both need and that refusal to allow discovery would prejudice or cause extreme hardship to him. Hickman v. Taylor (S.Ct.1947). The person requesting discovery must be able to show that there are no alternative means of obtaining the information and that it is vital to the preparation of the case. Several states have enacted the work-product rule as part of their discovery statutes, and the Hickman rule is now incorporated in the federal rules. See Fed. Rule 26(b)(3).

Some problems have arisen in defining what constitutes work-product. First, does it cover material gathered by persons other than the attorney, such as photographs or a surveillance report by an investigative agency? Second, is it limited to materials gathered solely in anticipation of trial or might it protect matter collected before it was reasonable to assume suit would be brought? The federal discovery rule attempts to answer these questions for the federal courts. It provides protection for all materials collected by the attorney or the attorney's agent and is limited to material gathered in anticipation of trial. Matter falling within this definition may be discovered only upon a showing of substantial need and undue hardship.

Instead of absolutely prohibiting the disclosure of any mental impressions of the attorney, as is done in some state rules, the federal rules provide that the court must guard against the disclosure of that matter. This difference still recognizes that the highest degree of protection must be given to mental impressions, but it allows the court to order response to a discovery request when the information sought is necessary for the requesting party and can be provided in a way that will protect the attorney's impressions of the case.

One unique feature of the federal rule is the exception that it contains allowing witnesses and parties to obtain their own statements, made at an earlier time, without showing any need or prejudice. This exception is designed to allow a witness to avoid the potential embarrassment of being confronted at trial with inconsistent statements made earlier. It was not part of the common law Hickman rule and many state rules that otherwise have followed the federal approach have not adopted this exception on the ground that the concerns underlying it are unwarranted.

Finally, the difference between attorney work-product protections and attorney-client privilege should be noted. The latter prohibits access to information communicated by the client to the attorney during the course of their confidential relationship. The client's information need not be given to the attorney in anticipation of actual litigation, but may be divulged merely in order to seek legal advice. There are no exceptional circumstances allowing access.

In the large corporate context, in which corporate counsel regularly consults and is consulted by numerous employees about various aspects of the business, it often becomes very important to identify when counsel merely is gathering information because of anticipated litigation and therefore may claim only the limited work-product protection, and when the attorney has obtained information under a pledge of confidentiality and for the identified purpose of giving legal advice so that the absolute privilege may be invoked. See, e.g., Upjohn Co. v. United States (S.Ct.1981). Merely transferring all internal corporate documents to the general counsel's office is not sufficient to qualify for protection.

§ 3–32. Expert Witnesses

Discovery involving expert witnesses poses special problems. At the outset they appear protected by the work-product rule because it may be only through the ingenuity and hard work of the attorney that the expert witnesses were uncovered and their testimony developed for the case. Further, discovery of these witnesses may reveal in substantial part the theories and conclusions of the side retaining them. On the other hand, because of the complex or technical nature of most expert testimony, there is a definite need for the opposing side to have some idea of what to expect so as to be able to cross-examine adequately and introduce an effective rebuttal. Concerns about fair and effective trials appear to outweigh fears about parasitism in this context.

In recognition of the special nature of this problem, most discovery rules explicitly permit discovery of the name and the substance of the testimony of any expert retained for use at trial. Indeed, under 1993 amendments to the federal rules, parties now are required to disclose the identity of all trial experts, as well as to provide a written report including the expert's opinions and supporting reasons that will be offered at trial. See § 3–22, above. Most discovery rules also allow discovery of experts who are retained by counsel, but who will not testify at trial, if there are exceptional circumstances why the movant cannot obtain like evidence by other means. Fed.Rule 26(b)(4)(B). In this way one party cannot effectively control the case by retaining all the noted and available authorities in a field, using only those who support his client's case. To avoid a possible windfall to the requesting party who obtains discovery under this exception, the court is authorized to require that party to pay a portion of the fees and expenses related to the experts discovered.

The special expert rule does not cover all categories of experts. Experts who have an informal relationship with an attorney, acting merely as sources of information without being retained, fall within the general work-product rule. Similarly, in states not having a special expert rule, discovery will be governed by the work-product rule and permitted only when it would prejudice the requesting party to deny it. Finally, experts who also are employees of corporate parties and who were not hired for purposes of the particular litigation at hand are fully discoverable as witnesses by either side.

§ 3–33. Insurance Agreements

In most states the fact of insurance is not admissible at trial and direct actions are not permitted against insurance companies. Injured parties must sue the insured and then seek reimbursement. These limitations are designed to protect the insurance industry from possible inflated verdicts entered by juries influenced by the deep pocket of the insurer rather than the merits of the plaintiff's case. Nonetheless, most states authorize the injured party to obtain discovery of the defendant's insurance coverage and, in the federal courts, insurance is one of the things that must be disclosed at the outset. See Fed.Rule 26(a)(1)(D). Although not relevant to the trial, discovery is permitted in order to allow the parties an opportunity to assess adequately the settlement value of the case. While this information may result in tougher bargaining for larger settlements, it is felt that a fair settlement process requires full disclosure.

§ 3–34. Abuses and Proposals for Reform

The liberal, wide-open discovery rules used in most state and federal courts have accomplished much in the way of eliminating verdicts won primarily by surprise tactics. They also have been terribly abused. In particular, critics point to massive document discovery and countless, needless interrogatories. The constant overuse of these devices has resulted in raising substantially the cost of litigation. In many instances discovery has become a tool of delay and harassment. Large corporate parties can coerce settlements in suits by individuals by threatening them with long and involved discovery. Conversely, a corporation faced with enormous document demands or a ceaseless series of interrogatories may feel settlement is the only reasonable alternative. In either case, it is clear that justice is subverted insofar as discovery is used not to search out the truth, but to force settlement.

The ethics of these tactics should be seriously questioned. Attorneys are officers of the court as well as adversaries, and owe it the duty of seeking, not side-stepping, justice. Several judges, bar associations, and commentators have urged reforms to curb these abuses. Suggestions range from limiting the quantity of discovery to returning to special pleading and simultaneously limiting the scope of discovery.

In the 1980s, the trend in federal discovery reform was away from precise limits and hard and fast rules and toward adding means by which the judges could control abuses. The federal discovery rules were amended in 1980 and 1983 to require discovery conferences, Fed.Rule 26(f), and to encourage the greater use of protective orders and sanctions to deter marginal practices. See § 3–30, above. An attorney signature requirement also was added to further encourage lawyers to consider the propriety of their requests and responses. Fed.Rule 26(g). Despite these changes, criticisms continue in the 1990s and more recent reforms have attempted to reduce the adversary character of some discovery by mandating early disclosure of certain information. See § 3–22, above. Additionally, absolute limits on the number of interrogatories and depositions in the absence of a court order have been introduced into both the federal and several state discovery rules. The likely success of these reforms remains unclear and further changes most likely will appear as courts grapple with how to achieve an appropriate information exchange without abusive litigation tactics.

E. PRETRIAL CONFERENCE

§ 3–35. In General

Because of the increased liberalization of pleading requirements, the pretrial conference has become the point in time at which the case becomes crystallized and structured. The conference typically occurs after discovery, when counsel, talking informally with the judge, are able to agree as to what issues are in dispute. They can plan the course of the trial because they know what evidence and witnesses they intend to introduce. In complex litigation, a series of conferences may be used to schedule discovery and to structure the trial.

The judge has discretion to schedule a pretrial conference in both state and federal systems, although some courts have provided by local rules that conferences are mandatory in all cases. The question whether pretrial conferences should be mandatory or discretionary is tied to the perennial debate on their ultimate usefulness. In simple cases, is more time wasted in the conference than is saved at trial or is it really a means of coercing settlement? In complicated cases, are the trials actually simplified and better organized and therefore speedier or does the pretrial conference merely add another hurdle and more time to the case?

In recognition of the frequent complexity of modern litigation and that leaving solely to the attorneys the responsibility to organize and move along their cases has not been satisfactory, the federal courts have been moving toward increased judicial management at the pretrial stage. In 1983, Federal Rule 16 was entirely rewritten to encourage federal judges to manage the cases before them, utilizing the pretrial conference to schedule the pretrial process, including discovery and motions, and thus to keep apprised of the attorneys' progress in the case.

§ 3–36. The Judge's Role

It is truly the judge who controls the effectiveness of the pretrial conference. The judge's interest, familiarity with the case, and belief as to the need to reach some agreement between the parties generally determines whether the parties actually will work toward some accord. The judge must tread a careful line between coercing the parties and helping them to reach reasonable conclusions. This problem has produced a difference of opinion as to whether the pretrial judge also should be assigned to try the case. If the pretrial and trial judges are different, then the expertise the judge gained during the pretrial is lost at trial. Conversely, the incentive of the pretrial judge to become totally familiar with the case is lessened, which may result in a less effective pretrial. On the other hand, using different trial and pretrial judges lessens the coerciveness of suggestions made by the pretrial judge; the parties need not fear that a failure to agree to some concession proposed by the judge will be prejudicial at trial. The pretrial judge functions more as an arbitrator or outside expert. At present, courts differ as to how they resolve this dilemma.

Regardless of whether the pretrial conference and trial are before the same judge, there are certain questions regarding the proper exercise of the judge's power at a pretrial conference that continue to surface. The first is the propriety of the judge urging the parties to settle the case out of court. Courts and commentators are split on this issue. Most judges seem to feel that it is proper to suggest that a settlement may be appropriate once the actual issues are revealed, and that one of the purposes of the conference is to see if an agreement can be reached and trial avoided. However, it is improper to coerce the parties into the settlement. The problem is one of degree. This view essentially is embraced in the federal rules, which specifically include in the objectives of pretrial conferences the desire to facilitate the settlement of the case. Fed. Rule 16(a)(5). Further, the judge may require that someone with settlement authority be available during the pretrial conference. Fed.Rule 16(c).

The second issue regarding judicial power concerns whether the judge may force the parties to stipulate as to the issues. One of the purposes of the conference is to formulate the issues for trial, stipulating as to agreed-upon non-issues. However, if a party refuses to concede that something is a non-issue, should the court be able to force the stipulation? Most courts answer no; the court may require the parties to enter a formal stipulation only when they agree on specific issues.

The final question involving the pretrial judge's power concerns what sanctions may be applied if the parties fail to appear at the conference or refuse or fail to reveal certain information requested by the court, such as the witnesses who will be called or the evidence that will be introduced at trial. It generally is recognized that the court may enter a default judgment or, in the case of a delinquent plaintiff, an involuntary dismissal with prejudice against parties whose counsel fail to appear at a scheduled conference. However, this sanction is so powerful that, as a practical matter, its use is strictly limited to situations in which the party has been exceptionally dilatory. This usually means that the counsel not only has failed to appear at the conference, but also generally has delayed the course of the litigation. A more common sanction is to limit the evidence to be used at trial to only that which was revealed at the conference pursuant to the court's request. Typically, the issue arises in the context of a motion to amend the pretrial order and the court's "sanction" for the earlier failure is to deny that motion. Federal Rule 16(f) expands on these traditional sanctions by including that the judge *must* require the party or attorney who failed to appear at a conference or otherwise did not cooperate as required under the rule to pay the expenses, including attorney fees, incurred by the opposing party as a result of that noncompliance, unless the court finds that the failure was substantially justified.

§ 3–37. Pretrial Orders

At the conclusion of the pretrial conference, the judge enters a pretrial order incorporating all the parties' stipulations, the list of witnesses and evidence agreed upon, and any other matters that were decided at the conference. The order supersedes the pleadings and controls the remainder of the proceedings in that action. If the attorneys wish to introduce a new issue or additional evidence at trial, they must petition the court for relief. Relief will be allowed to prevent manifest injustice, but it is within the discretion of the court to require adherence to its original order. Thus, the trial judge will weigh carefully the possible prejudice to the opposing party (who may have relied on the order when preparing for trial), the importance of the proposed change, and whether the moving party was dilatory in not introducing the proposed matter at the conference. If the movant succeeds, the relief typically will take the form of an amendment to the pretrial order.

CHAPTER IV

ADJUDICATION WITHOUT TRIAL

A. SUMMARY JUDGMENT

§ 4–1. In General

Summary judgment is a procedure by which a party can obtain a final binding determination on the merits without the necessity of a full trial. It differs from trial motions, such as the directed verdict, which also result in a final judgment, primarily because it is made earlier. A motion for summary judgment is distinguished from other pretrial motions to dismiss, demurrers or motions for judgment on the pleadings because outside evidence is produced and the court is not limited to the pleadings in making its decision. Indeed, it is common for the rules governing demurrers or motions for failure to state a claim for relief to provide that, if the movant introduces outside matter, the motion automatically is converted into one for summary judgment. A wide variety of outside material may be used, including affidavits, depositions, admissions and even interrogatories. The key in deciding whether the material is properly before the court is whether it would be admissible under the rules of evidence at trial.

157

Although the main purpose of summary judgment is to avoid unnecessary trials, it also can function to simplify the trial. Most judicial systems provide for some form of partial or interlocutory summary judgment by which only liability may be determined summarily or certain issues or claims may be eliminated from the case on summary judgment. See, e.g., Fed.Rules 56(c), (d). In addition, a party may move for summary judgment in order to force his opponent to reveal some of his case in resisting the motion.

Although summary judgment obviates the need for a trial, it does not impinge upon any jury trial rights. This is because the standard for obtaining summary judgment requires in part a finding that there is no fact issue to send to the jury, see § 4–2, below. The court does not weigh the evidence and decide that one party necessarily would succeed if the case went to a jury. Rather, it determines that there are no factual questions for the jury to decide and that therefore summary judgment is warranted.

§ 4–2. Grounds for Obtaining

The grounds for obtaining a summary judgment are threefold: there must be no *genuine issue* of *material fact* and the movant must be entitled to a judgment *as a matter of law*. See Fed.Rule 56(c). A party cannot resist a summary judgment motion simply by suggesting she is in disagreement with the movant's statement of facts. There must be a genuine or real dispute over certain factual issues. This typically requires the opposing party to introduce contradictory evidence, not merely to make conflicting allegations or arguments. Further, the facts in dispute must be central or material to the case. Disputes over irrelevant or minor facts will not bar summary judgment because, by definition, their determination will not affect the outcome even if a trial is had. Finally, the law governing the case must mandate a judgment for the movant given the undisputed facts. If any one of these three criteria is not met, the motion will be denied and the case sent to trial.

§ 4–3. Burden of Proof

A very important factor on summary judgment motions is the placement of the burden of proof. The movant necessarily has the initial burden of showing that the summary judgment standard has been met. This is true regardless of who would bear the burden of proof at trial. Most commonly, that burden is met by introducing outside evidence. In general, that evidence is viewed in the light most favorable to the opposing party. Even with that rule of interpretation, the movant often may have shown sufficient grounds for obtaining summary judgment.

In cases in which the opposing party would bear the burden of proof at trial, the party moving for summary judgment also may succeed by claiming that the opponent has no or insufficient evidence to satisfy its ultimate trial burden. See Celotex Corp. v. Catrett (S.Ct.1986). Exactly what the movant must do to show there is no evidence in support of the nonmovant's claim remains a bit unclear, however.

The one thing that is clear is that when determining whether to grant the motion, the court will evaluate the evidence in light of the substantive evidentiary standard of proof that will pertain at trial. For example, in a libel suit requiring actual malice to be proved in order to recover, defendant will prevail on a summary judgment unless there is sufficient evidence to establish a genuine issue of fact under the clear and convincing evidence standard, rather than the more general preponderance of the evidence standard. See Anderson v. Liberty Lobby, Inc. (S.Ct.1986).

Another important question that arises is what burdens are placed on the nonmovant to be able to successfully resist the motion. In some state systems it is permissible for the opposing party merely to rest on the well-pleaded allegations in his pleadings, noting the conflict between them and the movant's evidence. See, e.g., Cal.Civ.Proc.Code § 437c. This approach places a very minimal burden on the opposing party and, as a practical matter, means that summary judgment is almost impossible to obtain, except when the movant is resting her motion on the presence of an affirmative defense not rebutted by the pleadings.

In the federal courts, and in several state courts, the opposing party is not permitted to survive summary judgment on the basis of his pleadings, alone, unless the movant did not meet the initial burden of showing the absence of any genuine issue of fact. If the movant's papers show that no genuine issue of material fact exists, then the burden shifts to the opposing party to introduce outside evidence rebutting this conclusion, see Fed.Rule 56(e). If the opposing party fails to introduce any outside evidence, then the movant's evidence will be taken as true and in most cases this will result in summary judgment being granted. This approach of shifting the burden of proof to the opposing party was adopted so that summary judgment could act to pierce the pleadings and allow the court to assess the proof. To ameliorate some of the burden on the nonmovant, another provision authorizes him to meet that burden by showing why he is unable at that time to present evidence in opposition, see Fed.Rule 56(f). If the court finds those reasons to be valid, it may deny or postpone summary judgment.

§ 4–4. Credibility as a Fact Issue

One of the most difficult problems on a motion for summary judgment is when to allow a party to overcome an otherwise properly supported summary judgment motion on the ground that material facts will have to be proven by the testimony of witnesses whose credibility can be determined only by a jury. To the extent that this argument is accepted without reservation, summary judgment is almost impossible to obtain if any of the key evidence introduced on the motion consists of depositions or affidavits of witnesses or parties.

The decision to deny summary judgment when a credibility issue is raised varies from system to system and even from judge to judge, depending, at least in part, on the level of their concern that the procedure not be allowed to impinge on jury trial rights. In some states a specific provision exists in the summary judgment rule granting the court discretion to deny summary judgment whenever "the only proof of a material fact offered in support of the summary judgment is an affidavit or declaration made by an individual who was the sole witness to such fact." Cal.Civ.Proc.Code § 437c. This type of provision tips the balance in favor of a full trial. There is no comparable provision in the federal rules and the federal courts generally have held that an unsupported allegation that credibility is in issue will not suffice to overcome summary judgment. The party opposing summary judgment must introduce facts showing why a witness' credibility is in question. This typically requires evidence that the witness is not disinterested (i.e., is a party) or that the determination of an issue of fact rests on the state of mind or motive of the actor so that it ultimately must turn on that person's credibility as to what was in his mind at a given time. The court will not weigh or assess the actual credibility of any witness—that is the jury's role. Rather, it will decide if there is reason to believe that credibility may be determinative and if it finds that to be the case, then summary judgment will be denied.

§ 4–5. Procedure

Although the exact timing of summary judgment motions varies in each judicial system, a few general observations about the procedure on these motions can be made. Any party may move for summary judgment; cross-motions are possible. In that event, the court decides each motion separately. The fact that both parties are seeking summary judgment does not establish that there is no genuine issue of material fact.

In some situations, the court's review of the papers submitted in connection with one party's summary judgment motion will reveal that although there are no genuine, material factual issues, as a matter of law judgment should be for the opposing party. Although some courts have been reluctant to grant summary judgment under these circumstances, the clear trend supports the judge's authority to do so. However, the court must make certain that the party against whom judgment is to be entered had a full opportunity to present additional information showing what factual issues exist. The same problem of surprise is presented in an even more heightened fashion when the court decides on its own that summary judgment may be appropriate. Although several courts have been reluctant to enter summary judgment without a motion by at least one of the parties, as long as the opposing party is given a full opportunity to show why the summary judgment standard is not met, the court may enter judgment even without any formal motion.

Typically, there will be a summary judgment hearing, although this may not be required and the court may decide the motion on the basis of the papers, alone. If there is a hearing, the parties will be allowed to engage in oral argument supporting their positions.

B. DEFAULT JUDGMENT

§ 4–6. Types of Default

There are essentially three types of defaults. In the first, the defendant never appears or answers in response to the plaintiff's complaint. In the second, the defendant makes an appearance, but fails to file a formal answer or appear at trial. Both of these situations are specifically dealt with in specially designed rules present in each court system. In the third, the defendant fails to comply with some court order during the pretrial proceedings and the court enters a default judgment as a penalty. Authority for penalty defaults may be found in most discovery rules and they have been recognized as part of the inherent equitable power of the court to force compliance or cooperation at the pretrial discovery and conference stage.

The denomination of a particular case as falling into one of these three default situations has important consequences on the procedure that is utilized for obtaining the judgment, see § 4–7, below, and the party's ability to set aside the judgment, see § 6–1, below. However, all three situations have the same impact on the defendant, insofar as they all treat the default as a concession on liability. The immediate effect of a ruling that a default is involved typically is to find for the plaintiff on the merits.

§ 4–7.　Procedure

When the defendant defaults at the outset of a case and the plaintiff moves for the entry of a default, one of two procedures applies. If a sum certain (i.e., liquidated damages) is being sought, the clerk may enter a default. If not, the judge must enter the default and hold a hearing at which plaintiff will be required to prove the amount of damages, not liability. The plaintiff's ad damnum sets the ceiling on damages, but does not guarantee that that amount will be recovered. The defendant may appear at the damages hearing and may demand a jury trial on damages. This right is largely chimerical, however, because the defendant is not given any formal notice of the damages hearing and thus typically will not appear.

When the defendant has made an appearance and then defaulted, only the court may enter a default judgment and notice must be sent to the defendant prior to the damages hearing. Further, defendant has the right to have all the subsequent papers in the action served on him. A failure to send the prescribed notice is an automatic ground for setting aside the judgment. The damages hearing is the same as in the case of a default by nonappearance. The rationale for including a mandatory notice requirement in this situation is that the defendant has shown some interest in the litigation by making the initial appearance. Thus, the later default may have occurred as a result of the lawyer's failure to comply with various procedural provisions, rather than as a result of the conscious decision of the party. The notice provides some protection against this occurrence and further assures the defaulting party the opportunity of making a timely appeal.

The defendant may be found to have appeared and defended, not defaulted as, for example, if the defendant participates in the pretrial, but simply does not show up for trial. In that event special notice that a judgment is about to be entered need not be sent. Further, a motion to reopen the judgment and have a trial on the merits often will be viewed less favorably than it would if a default were involved. This is because, unlike true defaults, the issues have been framed in an adversary fashion and judgment will be entered only after the court has had an opportunity to evaluate the strength of the plaintiff's case on liability, as well as on damages, albeit that there will be only an ex parte presentation of the evidence. See generally § 6–1, below. Thus, it is important to determine what constitutes an appearance sufficient to invoke the default judgment rule's protections, but not so active as to be deemed a full defense.

In general, if the defendant files any pretrial motions short of an answer, or even more informally informs the court and opposing party of the intention to make an appearance, the court will treat the case as one in which the defendant has appeared and then defaulted. More difficult is the problem of how to treat the situation when defendant has filed a responsive pleading, but then failed to appear. On the one hand, defendant has placed the case in issue, not conceding liability, and the court should require the plaintiff to prove liability as well as damages before rendering judgment. On the other hand, because the defendant is not present at the trial, there is not a truly adversarial proceeding and perhaps the court should treat it as a default with liability conceded and hold a hearing on damages after notice has been sent to the defendant. Not surprisingly, the courts are split on this issue. If calling the defendant's failure to be present at trial a default will provide grounds for reopening the judgment, the answer frequently will be deemed an appearance and the defendant's subsequent conduct a default.

The penalty default situation has posed special procedural concerns for the courts. Some courts have treated it as a default after an appearance. Others have ruled it outside those protections. Most important is not the notice because the court in ordering the penalty to be imposed typically notifies the parties. Rather, whether the court can rule that the defendant has conceded the entire case—liability and damages—and whether the court can award the plaintiff in excess of the ad damnum as a penalty present more pressing issues. If the situation is treated as falling within the general default provisions, the answer to both of these questions is no, whereas it is yes, if it is not within those protections. The courts are split on these matters and the Supreme Court to date has not ruled on them.

C. VOLUNTARY AND INVOLUNTARY DISMISSAL

§ 4–8. Voluntary Dismissals

All judicial systems provide some means by which a plaintiff may voluntarily dismiss the case without court approval. This may occur when upon further investigation the plaintiff determines that she really does not have a claim worth pursuing or when the parties have settled the suit out of court. Countervailing considerations suggest that some limitations be placed on this procedure. People should be encouraged to file suit only when they are serious about pursuing the case to judgment. Unrestricted voluntary dismissals would allow plaintiffs to harass defendants and present serious potential for abuse.

The federal rules provide the plaintiff only one automatic right to a voluntary dismissal without prejudice. See Fed.Rule 41(a). If the same suit is filed again and another voluntary dismissal is sought and granted, it will be entered with prejudice, thereby preventing the action from being filed a third time. Further, the plaintiff can voluntarily dismiss an action after the defendant has answered only with the consent of the defendant or by obtaining court approval. Similar restrictions exist in most state provisions.

§ 4–9. Involuntary Dismissals: Failure to Prosecute

A court can enter an involuntary dismissal for failure to prosecute. The defendant typically moves for this dismissal on the ground that plaintiff has failed to take appropriate steps to move the case to trial, has failed to appear at scheduled hearings or conferences, or continually has delayed or sought continuances to lengthen normal time periods. If the court grants the motion, the case will be dismissed with prejudice on the merits, unless the court specifically stipulates otherwise—a very rare occurrence. Thus, involuntary dismissals are granted sparingly and usually only when the plaintiff has been particularly dilatory and the delay has resulted in prejudice to the defendant.

Some provisions, such as Federal Rule 41(b), leave the decision to enter an involuntary dismissal totally within the discretion of the trial court. Others, such as the California Code, give some further direction to the court, permitting a dismissal only two years after the filing of the complaint and mandating dismissal when five years of inactivity or dilatoriness is shown. Within that period, the court can exercise its discretion to determine if the plaintiff's lack of action amounts to a total failure to prosecute. Cal.Civ.Proc.Code § 583.

CHAPTER V

THE TRIAL

A. THE PROCESS

§ 5–1. A General Description

Once a case has proceeded through discovery and survived any pretrial motions that may have been made, it will be placed on the court's trial docket and a date for trial assigned. At that time, if no continuances or postponements occur, the parties and their counsel must appear to begin the trial.

Both jury and non-jury trials follow the same general pattern, although the outset of the trial differs in a jury case as time must be spent choosing a jury to sit in the case. See § 5–9, below. The order of presentation may vary slightly from court to court, but the general rules are as follows. Plaintiff's counsel followed by defendant's attorney each make opening statements, explaining what they intend to prove. The plaintiff's witnesses and evidence are examined and cross-examined. Then the defendant's witnesses and evidence are introduced, with similar rights of examination and cross-examination. The plaintiff and defendant then may be allowed to introduce rebuttal evidence. After all the evidence has been submitted, each side makes closing arguments summarizing the evidence supporting their respective positions. Plaintiff again typically summarizes first, but has a right of rebuttal after the defendant's closing remarks have been made. If there is no jury, the judge then will evaluate the evidence and render a judgment. If a jury is present, the judge instructs the jurors as to the law to be applied. Most commonly, the judge will require the parties to submit possible instructions in advance and will choose from among those submissions. In some jurisdictions, pattern instructions have been approved for various types of legal issues and the parties will not need to prepare special drafts for their particular cases. In a few jurisdictions and in the federal courts the judge also may comment on the evidence. However, in most states this is deemed improper and the judge is authorized only to give an impartial summary of the evidence.

The jury then retires to deliberate in order to render its verdict. If the jurors report that they are deadlocked, the judge may send them back for additional deliberations. But if that fails to break the deadlock, a mistrial will have to be declared. If the jury returns with a verdict, the judge will enter a judgment on it.

§ 5–2. Rules of Evidence

The trial process is governed by rules of evidence. Each court system has its own set of evidentiary rules and the character of the trial may vary somewhat depending on what types of evidence are permitted to be introduced. Most generally, proper evidence or testimony is that which is relevant and not privileged or hearsay. Definitions of relevance, privilege, and hearsay fill the law books and are explored more fully in the separate course on evidence. A brief description here will suffice.

The relevance of specific evidence is determined in relation to the scope of the issues in the case. Irrelevant evidence is excluded in order to aid the trier of fact in focusing on what actually is in issue. Privileged matter is excluded to protect the privacy of individuals in certain relationships (e.g., doctor-patient, lawyer-client). Persons in a privileged relationship need not reveal any communications that occurred between them. The law places a greater value on preserving the sanctity of those relationships than on the need to determine the truth based on all the possible evidence. Hearsay is defined as an out-of-court statement offered to prove the fact or truth of the matter stated. The rules defining hearsay are riddled with exceptions. In general, the prohibition against the use of hearsay evidence exists because hearsay is deemed inherently unreliable because there is no opportunity to cross-examine the actual person who made the statement. The exceptions that are recognized typically involve situations in which other circumstances appear to ensure that the evidence is reliable (such as the exception for the introduction of records created during the day-to-day operation of a business), or in which there does not appear to be other evidence that could be used to prove the matter at issue (such as statements by a person regarding his motives).

Counsel must raise evidentiary objections immediately or they will be waived. In addition, in the case of privileged information, the parties to the relationship can waive their right to claim privilege by their conduct. If an objection is sustained, the evidence will be stricken or the jury will be instructed not to take it into account in rendering the verdict. However, there often is a serious question whether it is reasonable to expect the jurors to disregard improper evidence that is mentioned in their presence, even if instructed to do so, or whether the jury has been so prejudiced that a mistrial should be called. In contrast, a judge trial often is less rigid in adhering strictly to the evidentiary rules and fewer evidentiary objections are raised because it is assumed that the judge will disregard improper evidence and consider only proper evidence.

B. JURY TRIAL

1. IN GENERAL

§ 5–3. The Jury—Its History, Character and Function

Jury trial is a fundamental part of the Anglo–American dispute resolution process. It was first formalized in the Twelfth Century in England during the reign of King Henry II and it fast became the hallmark of the common law courts. The historic jury was composed of twelve men from the community. These men were asked to determine what were the actual facts underlying a controversy and the judge then would apply the law. The jury's decision had to be unanimous. Although the form of the jury remained the same when it was transplanted to the American colonies, it assumed additional meanings. Jury trial became a symbol of American freedom or popular justice versus the king's justice. Even though the need to establish our independence has long since passed, jury trial remains at the core of the civil court system.

Several state and federal courts have modified the original character of the jury to allow juries composed of less than twelve members, as well as the use of non-unanimous verdicts. These changes have been in an effort to reduce the costliness of jury trials. Smaller juries should be selected more rapidly, and their deliberations should be shorter simply because there are fewer individual opinions to consider. Non-unanimous verdicts lessen the possibility of a deadlock, with its attendant need for a new trial. The United States Supreme Court upheld the use of six member juries in civil cases, Colgrove v. Battin (S.Ct.1973), and non-unanimous verdicts in criminal cases, Apodaca v. Oregon (S.Ct. 1972) against challenges that these changes violated the jury trial guarantee in the Constitution. It has not yet ruled on non-unanimous civil verdicts, but its reasoning in the criminal field suggests that they also would be upheld. The Court ruled that the character of the jury trial was not part of the historic or constitutional right and that, based on the studies to date, it could find no proof of a qualitative difference between verdicts rendered under either system. Thus, the lower courts are left to decide for themselves whether to modify the twelve person, unanimous jury, and the character of the jury may vary depending on the court in which suit is brought.

The role of the jury remains unchanged, however. The jury is to decide questions of fact; the judge determines issues of law. This distribution of responsibility recognizes the special qualities of the jury and the judge. The jury is present to conform legal standards to current experience. For example, if a case involves the interpretation of a contract, a question of fact is presented and a jury decision on the meaning of certain contract language relies on community experience as to common practices when persons enter into a contract. The judge's role is to provide rules to bind litigants in the future so that the community can know how to conduct future dealings. In contract disputes the judge decides whether a legally binding or valid contract has been made. The jury decides all issues of credibility since those are questions of fact, but the judge determines if the law allows relief under the facts as determined by the jury.

The line between issues of fact and of law is not always easy to ascertain and the case reports are filled with cases in which judges improperly have removed issues from the jury. The appropriate delineation of the jury's role is clouded further because of the jury nullification process. Most often, the judge instructs the jury on the law applicable to a given set of facts and the jury not only determines the facts, but also applies the law to those facts. (See § 5–10, below, on types of verdicts.) In areas where the law has been slow to develop, the jury may decide to dispense justice, ignoring the law. Illustratively, there are negligence cases in which it is quite clear that the jury ignored rules of contributory negligence that would bar plaintiff's recovery and simply took the plaintiff's negligence into account in assessing the damages—utilizing a comparative negligence standard before it was adopted by the courts. Jury proponents argue that this is one of the special functions of the jury and is simply a means of modernizing the law in light of current community mores. However, allowing the jury to tamper with the law presents potential dangers in situations, such as in the civil rights field, in which local community standards are inconsistent with more general, indeed constitutional, national standards. For these reasons, all judicial systems contain some devices by which the judge is given power to control the jury and prevent it from acting improperly. These devices are explored in later sections. See §§ 5–8—5–11, below.

2. SCOPE OF JURY TRIAL RIGHTS

§ 5–4. Sources of Jury Trial Rights

The right to a jury trial in a civil action may derive from one of three sources. The first, and broadest, is constitutional. Federal and state constitutions set the minimal standards for jury trial in their respective judicial systems. The legislature has the power to authorize jury trial in cases not within the constitutional guarantee. Thus, the second jury trial source is statutory and represents those situations in which the legislature in establishing a particular cause of action has granted a right to a jury trial. Finally, the trial court always has the equitable power to impanel a jury, although in those instances the jury will be advisory only and the judge may accept or disregard its findings.

The major problems in determining the scope of jury trial rights have been in the constitutional area. It should be noted that the federal constitutional jury provision (Seventh Amendment) is not binding on the states so that states have been free to develop their own scheme of civil jury trial rights for their courts. All but four of the states (Colorado, Utah, Louisiana, and Wyoming) have constitutional provisions similar to the federal and in those four states statutory jury trial rights exist. Further, with the exception of four other states (Georgia, North Carolina, Tennessee, and Texas), which provide a jury trial in equity, all the states appear to interpret their constitutional and statutory provisions similarly to the federal courts in that they determine the right to jury trial based on whether that right would have existed at the time the governing constitutional provision was adopted. Thus, the following discussion will explore civil jury trial rights in the federal courts as that provides the best model for study.

§ 5–5. Constitutional Juries in Nonstatutory Actions

The Seventh Amendment to the United States Constitution provides for a right to jury trial "in suits at common law" exceeding twenty dollars. Thus, the test for determining whether the Seventh Amendment is properly invoked requires an inquiry into history and whether the action was one that could have been brought at common law, rather than in an equity court. This inquiry can be most complex because separate equity and law courts no longer exist; the federal courts now are empowered to try all claims. Further, the availability of joinder of claims and parties under modern rules of procedure presents situations unknown at common law.

In essence, the Supreme Court has developed the following approach to how to apply the Seventh Amendment guarantee in modern cases. The right to a jury trial depends on the nature of the *issue* on which a jury trial is demanded. If the underlying nature of the issue is legal, then it does not matter that the type of proceeding involved (i.e., class or derivative suits or interpleader proceedings) historically was available only in equity. A jury trial is required on that issue. Ross v. Bernhard (S.Ct. 1970). Further, it does not matter whether the legal issue is introduced by way of the plaintiff's claim or by the defendant's answer, it requires a jury trial. In cases in which there is a common factual issue to both a legal and an equitable claim, that issue must be tried first by the jury, before the judge can rule on the equitable claim. Beacon Theatres, Inc. v. Westover (S.Ct.1959).

Focusing on the issue rather than the action as a whole and ordering the trial to permit a jury trial on any common factual issues prior to deciding the equitable claims represents a definite departure from history. Traditionally, the equity clean-up doctrine provided that in suits first properly lodged in equity, the judge would determine any incidental legal issues. The Supreme Court has specifically rejected the clean-up doctrine, exhibiting a definite preference for jury trial. Not all the states have followed this approach in interpreting their own provisions. The basis for this movement away from a rigid historical test is the Court's belief that the availability of new legal remedies necessarily reduces the scope of equity, which was developed to apply only when there were no adequate legal remedies. Under the current standard, history alone does not reveal whether an action will be deemed a "suit at common law" for Seventh Amendment purposes. Rather, the court must determine whether changes in the availability of legal remedies and procedures have made it unnecessary to resort to equity so that the claim or issue involved now properly may be characterized as legal and within the scope of the constitutional jury trial guarantee.

This same flexible approach appears in the current standard for determining the legal nature of an issue. The historical treatment of an issue still is important. For example, fraud remains equitable and no jury trial right attaches. Further, the remedy being sought aids in deciding whether a jury is required so that suits seeking only injunctive relief, being traditionally equitable, should not require a jury. However, the form of relief is not always determinative and, once again, if new applicable legal remedies exist, the claim may be treated as legal. For example, a claim for an accounting was deemed legal for jury trial purposes because the availability of masters to assist the jury removed the traditional reason for referring those claims to equity and the judge. Dairy Queen, Inc. v. Wood (S.Ct.1962).

In a footnote in one opinion, the Supreme Court also suggested that a proper consideration in deciding whether a jury trial should be used may be the "practical abilities and limitations of juries." Ross v. Bernhard (S.Ct.1970). To date the Court has not explained how this last factor may be utilized, although the reference to jury limitations suggests that in some instances it might serve to narrow jury rights. Thus, it has been argued that there may be a complexity exception to the Seventh Amendment—if the court finds that certain litigation is so complex that a jury could not practically decide the issues, it may determine that there is no constitutional right to a jury trial, using this last factor. The Supreme Court has not ruled on this question and the lower courts are divided on it.

§ 5–6. Constitutional Juries in Statutory Actions

In most cases the fact that an action is statutory does not determine whether the Seventh Amendment applies. If Congress specifically provides for jury trial, then the constitutional question need not be reached. In the absence of a statutory jury trial right, the right to a jury trial will depend on whether the issues involved in presenting a claim under the statute are legal or equitable in nature. Since the majority of liability statutes merely codify pre-existing common law rights, most statutory actions involve the same analytical jury trial problems as nonstatutory actions. See § 5–5, above.

An important issue peculiar to statutory actions does arise, however. That is whether the Congress can effectively declare something equitable and outside the scope of the Seventh Amendment, even though historically the issue would have received a jury trial in a suit at common law. Generally, if the statute involved provides for a statutory proceeding before an administrative board or a specialized court, rather than an action in a general district court, and if there is evidence supporting the need for non-jury treatment, the enactment will withstand constitutional attack. See Atlas Roofing Co. v. Occupational Safety & Health Review Comm'n (S.Ct.1977)(administrative tribunal); Katchen v. Landy (S.Ct.1966)(bankruptcy court); and NLRB v. Jones & Laughlin Steel Corp. (S.Ct.1937)(administrative tribunal). The answer is not so clear when the statute provides for trial in the general federal district courts.

In two cases decided by the Supreme Court in which an argument was raised that jury trial was inconsistent with congressional intent in the statutes on which the suits were based, the Court upheld the constitutional right to a jury trial, noting that the actions had common law analogs and the only arguments for non-jury trial were unsupported allegations that the jury would not function so as to do justice and that it was inconsistent with the policies underlying the enactments. See Curtis v. Loether (S.Ct.1974), (claim jury prejudice would undermine enforcement of civil rights act regulating housing discrimination), and Pernell v. Southall Realty (S.Ct.1974)(claim congressional intent to provide speedy remedy in landlord-tenant area inconsistent with use of jury trial). In both of these cases the arguments against jury trial rested on implied legislative intent. In contrast, in Tull v. United States (S.Ct.1987), the Court held that Congress could provide for a civil penalty to be assessed for violation of a statute and, although the jury would need to determine whether a penalty should be imposed, the amount of the penalty could be set by the judge in keeping with congressional intent. The Court has not yet ruled on the question whether clearly expressed congressional intent to create a statutory cause of action to be enforced in the courts without the availability of a jury trial is sufficient to place the action outside the scope of the Seventh Amendment. Of course, the constitutional presumption for jury trial is clear, and there always will be a heavy burden of proof on the legislature if it attempts to overcome it, requiring substantial and express reasons supporting the legislative preference for non-jury trial.

§ 5–7. Demand Requirements

In a few state courts, jury trial is used unless a non-jury trial is requested. In most states and in the federal system, the converse is true. Unless a jury trial is demanded within the statutory period, the right to trial by jury is waived. Although the court has the discretion to allow an untimely demand, that discretion is exercised sparingly and in most instances there is no relief from waiver.

Demand requirements have withstood constitutional challenge. They are not viewed as terribly burdensome to the parties and thus their impact on constitutional jury rights is minimal. That minimal effect is deemed justifiable because of the generally recognized need for the courts to be able to exercise some docket control. The ability to determine at an early stage whether an action requires a jury permits the courts to schedule their cases accordingly and in that way better administer their caseloads. Thus, it is important to check the specific demand requirements of the court in which suit is brought in order not to fail inadvertently to make a timely request.

3. MEANS OF CONTROLLING THE JURY

§ 5–8. In General

There are various methods or procedures designed to ensure that the jury performs its proper role. The evidentiary rules, for example, limit the jury to considering only legally relevant and generally reliable evidence in determining the facts. A judge who sustains objections to proposed evidence or testimony protects the jury from considering possibly irrelevant and prejudicial matters. (See § 5–2, above.) Similarly, the judge's instructions to the jury describe and define the proper scope of its inquiry, prescribing who has the burden of persuasion on the facts in issue. Of course, the effectiveness of this control depends totally on whether the jury follows the judge's charges. However, the attorneys may ask the judge to poll the jury after a verdict has been announced to make certain that each of the jurors is in agreement with and understands the verdict. Alternatively, the judge has the power to select the type of verdict that should be rendered, which may limit the jurors' ability to ignore the controlling law. (See § 5–10, below.) The following sections describe some of the means of jury control.

§ 5–9. Selection Process

Even though the actual jury selection process varies from court to court, a few generalized statements can be made. The process begins by notices sent to community members by the court clerk requesting them to appear and be placed in the jury pool (called the *array*). Some potential jurors may exclude themselves if they fit under statutory exceptions. Excuses from jury service usually are limited to vocational categories (e.g., firemen or doctors), to health reasons or to incompetence (e.g., cannot speak English). Jurors also may be excused if they can show that it would be an undue hardship for them to have to serve. Under the federal jury selection statutes, the procedures used to create the jury pool are designed to obtain a broad cross-section of the community. Although state jury systems are not required to develop processes fostering this cross-section concept, it is common to most systems. States are limited by the Fourteenth Amendment in designing their methods of jury selection, however. This means that no particular group can be systematically excluded, and that litigants must be afforded procedures within the selection process consistent with fundamental fairness.

Individual jurors from the array are selected to sit on a specific case (*panel*) after being examined before the court. That screening is called *voir dire*. In some courts the judge asks the jurors all questions; the attorneys submit in advance any questions they would like answered. In other courts the attorneys themselves conduct voir dire. The purpose under either approach is to determine if any prospective jurors are likely to be so biased or prejudiced in the case that they could not reach an independent judgment based on the facts presented. If so, the attorney may *challenge for cause* and, if the judge agrees, that person will be dis-

qualified.   If the judge permits the juror to remain,
the same challenge can be raised on appeal from
the final judgment and the verdict will be overturned if the trial court's decision was an abuse of
discretion.   Attorneys also are given a limited number of *peremptory challenges* by which they can
reject a potential juror without stating the reason.
This device allows the attorney to try to select
those persons most likely to be sympathetic to the
client or to the type of evidence that will be presented.   The attorney can reject persons who do
not reveal enough bias to merit a challenge for
cause, but that the attorney feels will be prejudiced
against the client or case.   By careful use of their
challenges, the attorneys shape the character of
each jury.   The only limitations on the use of peremptory challenges is that they cannot be used to
exclude jurors on the basis of their race because
doing so violates the constitutional rights of the
excluded jurors.   See Edmonson v. Leesville Concrete Co. (S.Ct.1991).

§ 5–10.   Types of Verdicts

There are three types of verdicts that may be
used.   The type of verdict used may help ensure
that the jury performs only its assigned function of
resolving issues of fact.

Most frequently a *general verdict* is requested.
The judge instructs the jury on the law and the jury
applies the law to the facts as it finds them, report-
ing to the court only which party wins and the
relief, if any, to be awarded.   Obviously, the general

verdict provides little jury control because there is no way to determine on what the verdict is based. Further, in the event of an appeal, the reviewing court must reverse if there has been an error involving any of the alternative claims, theories or defenses presented to the jury because it cannot be certain whether the jury rested its decision on findings supported by improper evidence or on other grounds.

The *special verdict* is at the opposite end of the spectrum. The court requests the jury to make specific findings of fact and the judge applies the law to those facts and renders judgment accordingly. The special verdict is designed to make the trial process more scientific and prevents the jury from acting on bias or ignoring the law. In this way, the number of appellate reversals should be reduced. The device has been criticized, however, because it makes the jury deliberation process much more difficult and slow. Additionally, the exercise of such tight control over the jury is challenged as inconsistent with the historic power of the jury to bring the community's standards to bear on a case, even when those mores differ from specific laws. Despite these objections, any party may request the court to use a special verdict or the court may decide on its own to do so. It is totally within the discretion of the trial judge whether to utilize a special verdict.

As a middle ground between special and general verdicts, the court may use a *general verdict with interrogatories*. The judge instructs the jury on the law and requests a general verdict as described above. Additionally, however, certain specific cross-check questions are submitted to enable the judge to determine whether the verdict rendered is consistent with the facts as found. The judge is not supposed to try to restrict the jury by including so many detailed questions that the jury has no discretion regarding the size or type of award rendered. Rather, the questions typically are designed to make certain that the liability determination is consistent with the facts—that the law was applied properly.

In addition to the difficulty in drafting clear and unambiguous questions to be sent to the jury, the use of a special verdict or a general verdict with interrogatories may present some problems for the court if the jury cannot or does not respond clearly to the inquiries made. The jury's findings generally must be unambiguous in order to allow the court to enter judgment on them, although the judge has a duty to try to harmonize any apparent inconsistencies when it is possible to do so. In the case of a general verdict with interrogatories, specific rules usually outline the options for a judge when the answers to the interrogatories do not support the verdict. If the answers are internally consistent, but simply cannot be reconciled with the verdict, the judge is authorized to return the case to the jury for further consideration, to enter a verdict consistent with the specific answers, or to set the case for a new trial. If some of the answers are not consistent internally, as well as contrary to the verdict, then the judge's options are to return the case to the jury or order a new trial. See Fed.Rule 49(b). The choice of which option to use is within the court's discretion, and typically will depend on the judge's perception of whether the jury is so confused that further deliberations merely might mask jury error.

§ 5–11. Impeachment of the Verdict

Although a verdict may appear proper on its face, a variety of circumstances may have occurred suggesting that the jury did not function properly and the judgment should be set aside. For example, the jurors may have considered evidence not introduced at the trial and thus not subject to examination and cross-examination. They may have visited the scene of the accident on their own or one of the jurors may have "testified" to the others on the matters in question. A juror may have failed to reveal during voir dire his or her relationship with one of the parties or their attorneys. The jury may not have reached a unanimous verdict on liability and damages, but instead may have used a quotient verdict with each member simply writing down the judgment felt to be fair and then dividing the sum total by the number of jury members. In any one of these or a number of other circumstances, the parties have been deprived of their right to a totally impartial, properly functioning jury, which considers only court controlled evidence and reaches a unanimous decision on the basis of that evidence alone.

A problem that exists in any of the above situations is what evidence may be introduced to prove juror misconduct to the possible prejudice of the losing party and thus to impeach the verdict. The sanctity and total privacy of jury deliberations has been seen as the best means of assuring a fair trial; it encourages the jurors to feel free to discuss and vote their conscience because they know that whatever takes place will not be revealed publicly. Thus, any evidence of juror misconduct that requires an inquiry into the deliberation process is suspect. Further, it is argued that there is no way to assure a completely impartial jury as each member necessarily brings to the trial certain individual feelings or predispositions; all that the jury process is trying to obtain is a cross-section of the community so that various prejudices will be counterbalanced. Finally, the cost of overturning the verdict because the jury did not act properly is to require an entire new trial with no assurance of reaching a more just result.

Given these arguments, it should not be surprising that the historic and most widely followed rule (the Mansfield rule) has been that juror affidavits regarding what occurred during their deliberations cannot be used to impeach the verdict. However, a verdict may be impeached on the basis of juror affidavits regarding misconduct prior to their deliberations, such as if one juror lied during voir dire regarding his prior relationship with one of the parties, or on the basis of evidence from other nonjury sources. For example, a person who observed the jury visiting the scene of the accident could testify to that effect in order to support an argument that the jury relied on evidence not presented to them at the trial.

Most jurisdictions today have attempted to ameliorate the harshness of the Mansfield rule by allowing the verdict to be challenged on the basis of juror testimony concerning overt acts of other jury members that may have been prejudicial. The impeaching evidence cannot rest on the state of mind or feelings of individual jurors, however. Under this approach, a verdict can be impeached on the basis of a juror affidavit to the effect that one of the members told the jury that she had a family emergency and urged them to reach a quick decision and terminate their discussion so that she could return home. An affidavit stating that one of the jurors had received news of a family emergency and had acted under great stress and hastily when reaching the verdict will not be allowed because it attempts to testify as to the motives and state of mind of that juror. Under the Mansfield rule, neither affidavit is permissible.

The federal courts have adopted a compromise position on this question. Federal Rule of Evidence 606 allows the introduction of juror testimony only to show that prejudicial outside evidence was brought into the jury room or extraneous influences were improperly brought to bear on any juror. The federal formulation thus avoids the problem of determining what constitutes an "act" and recognizes that a verdict can be tainted by any information.

However, it too precludes the use of testimony concerning the effect that information had on the jurors. The likelihood of prejudice must be determined objectively by the court.

C. TRIAL AND POST–TRIAL MOTIONS

§ 5–12. Directed Verdicts

Directed verdict motions (called motions for judgment as a matter of law in the federal system) may be made by either party at the close of their opponent's evidence. The theory behind the motion is that there is insufficient evidence to go to the jury or that the evidence is so compelling that only one result could follow, so that to save trial time the court should enter a judgment for the movant. Although the effect of a successful directed verdict motion is to take the case away from the jury, the Supreme Court has ruled that directed verdict motions do not violate the constitutional jury trial guarantee because comparable procedures—i.e., demurrers to the evidence—existed at common law. Galloway v. United States (S.Ct.1943).

The issue before the trial court on a directed verdict motion is whether there is sufficient evidence to raise a fact issue. In order to answer this question, the court will view the evidence in the light most favorable to the nonmovant. In a few jurisdictions this means that the judge will not consider the moving party's evidence. But this rule of construction makes it almost impossible to obtain a directed verdict. Thus, more commonly, the court will review all the evidence, deciding any credibility problems in favor of the nonmovant.

There are two different formulations of the standard for granting a directed verdict: the scintilla test and the substantial evidence test. Under the scintilla test the court will deny the motion and refer the case to the jury if there is a scintilla, or *any,* evidence on which the jury might possibly render a verdict for the nonmovant. Under the substantial evidence test, the court will grant the motion unless there is sufficient or substantial evidence suggesting that the jury might decide for the nonmovant. The difference between these two tests reflects the different attitudes that courts have with regard to the importance of jury trial and the amount of control that properly may be exercised by the judge over the jury. The modern trend has been toward the use of the substantial evidence test.

The application of either the scintilla or substantial evidence test involves a complex analysis of what evidence is necessary to prove a particular claim or defense, what are the permissible inferences to draw for gaps in the evidence, who has the burden of proof on the issues presented, and, in some cases, whether questions concerning the credibility of some of the witnesses require denial of the motion or may be evaluated against the background of the other evidence that was introduced. A discussion of these variables may be found in J. Friedenthal, M. Kane & A. Miller, *Civil Procedure* § 12.3 (2d ed.1993).

§ 5–13. Judgments Notwithstanding the Verdict

The major difference between a motion for judgment notwithstanding the verdict (JNOV) and a directed verdict motion is the timing. Indeed, since 1991, both motions have been called by the same name, motions for judgment as a matter of law, in the federal system to underscore their common identity. A JNOV motion is made to the trial judge after the verdict is rendered (usually within 10 days of the verdict) and seeks a judgment contrary to it on the ground that there was insufficient evidence for the jury to find as it did. Its primary use is when there is some overriding issue of law that indicates that the jury verdict is erroneous. The court deciding a JNOV motion does not weigh the evidence any more than it does on a directed verdict motion. Rather, it considers whether there was any evidence supporting the jury's verdict in light of the law governing the case.

The JNOV motion serves several important functions. At the outset its availability encourages the judge to ease back on the directed verdict motion. At the time of that earlier motion the judge may not be ready to decide whether the evidence is sufficient to warrant a judgment. The judge can submit the case to the jury, and in many cases the verdict will be the same as would have occurred on the directed verdict motion. When the judge's inclination and the jury's disposition agree, quarrels (and appeals) about directed verdicts cannot arise. When they disagree, the court still can impose its will. Additional time savings also occur in the event of an appeal. If a JNOV is reversed, the jury's verdict is entered. If a directed verdict is reversed, a new trial is necessary so that the case can be sent to a jury. This ultimate savings in trial time on JNOV may be offset, however, by the fact that more appeals may be taken from JNOV rulings than from directed verdicts because the difference between the judge and jury is only speculative in the directed verdict context.

In the federal courts, a motion for judgment as a matter of law can be made after the jury's verdict is rendered only if it is a renewal of the same motion made at the close of evidence and before the case was submitted to the jury. See Fed.Rule 50(b). This is because there is no historic common law analog for the post verdict motion. Those motions have withstood the challenge that they violate federal constitutional jury trial rights solely on the ground that they are delayed directed verdict motions and directed verdicts were authorized in common law actions. See § 5–12, above. Since the states are not bound by the Seventh Amendment, they are free to treat these two motions differently and several states allow JNOV motions to be made even though no directed verdict motion was interposed.

§ 5–14. New Trial

Judicial systems typically provide some means by which a party dissatisfied with the first proceeding may request a new trial. In this way, the trial judge is given an opportunity to correct any errors that may have occurred during the first trial. Under some rules, specific grounds, such as misconduct of the jury, newly discovered material evidence, or errors of law, are set out and automatically authorize the right to a new trial, see, e.g., Minn. Rules of Proc. 59.01. Under others, the trial court is allowed more discretion and is given the power to grant a new trial motion based on grounds "heretofore recognized," see, e.g., Fed. Rule 59(a). In either case, the discretion granted the judge to set aside the verdict and order a new trial is much greater than on a JNOV motion. In sum, the judge can consider any error of law in the trial that may have prejudiced the movant. The court may take into account prejudicial errors in rulings on the evidence or in the instructions to the jury, evidence of jury or attorney misconduct, newly discovered evidence, or the fact that the verdict is against the weight of the evidence. This last ground may merit relief even though the legal insufficiency of the evidence falls short of that required to support a directed verdict or JNOV motion.

The contrast between new trial and JNOV rulings sometimes appears shadowy, especially when the ground for new trial relates to the sufficiency of the evidence. But the difference is real. The evidence may be such that reasonable people could find as the jury found, precluding a JNOV, but the verdict still may be against the weight of the evidence, meriting a new trial. The resulting impact of an order granting a JNOV also differs sharply from that granting a new trial. The victim of a JNOV is denied the benefit of a favorable jury verdict; the victim of a new trial order complains that he gets too much jury trial, not too little.

The only real limitation imposed on a person moving for a new trial is time. Generally, new trial motions are governed by strict and short timing provisions (e.g., 10 days after the judgment is entered or the verdict is returned). The failure to move within the statutory period is fatal.

The trial judge's decision on a motion for new trial most frequently is controlling. In most judicial systems an immediate appeal cannot be taken from an order granting a new trial as it is interlocutory. This delays appellate review of the new trial order until after the second trial and its verdict, thereby decreasing substantially the likelihood of reversal. If the second proceeding lacks prejudicial errors, there typically is no justification for disregarding the judgment entered therein simply because the second trial was not necessary. It is difficult to determine which of two reasonable juries was most reasonable.

On an appeal from a ruling denying a new trial, the appellate court will reverse only if it finds an abuse of discretion. This seldom occurs on sufficiency of evidence grounds; the appellate court will find that the trial court abused its discretion when it determined that the evidence was sufficient to support the jury's verdict typically only when the trial judge was wrong as a matter of law as to the reasons that would support the grant or denial of the motion. In general the deference to the trial court shown by the appellate courts stems from the fact that, since the trial judge was present at the initial proceedings, he is likely to be in the best position to assess if any reasons exist that make suspect the verdict reached there. A few courts have suggested, however, that a broader review of the trial judge's action may be appropriate when a new trial is granted on the ground that the weight of the evidence was against the verdict. These cases reflect the concern that allowing the trial judge too much discretion could result in improper intrusions on the jury's decisionmaking authority.

§ 5–15. Partial and Conditional New Trials

In order to avoid the expense of an entire new trial, the judge may decide to order a new trial only on those issues tainted with error. Although a partial new trial may result in considerable savings, it also presents some potential problems. The court must make certain that the issues not retried are truly separable from those resubmitted. Otherwise, the second judgment will remain tainted by the error in the first trial. Indeed, the court generally should not order a partial new trial on liability alone. Jurors' attitudes toward liability frequently are reflected in the amount of damages they award and the issues are so intertwined that if there has been some error concerning the evidence directed toward liability, a new jury should consider both aspects of the case. Thus, most commonly partial new trials are ordered on the amount of damages, not on liability. A minority of courts have argued that partial new trials always are defective because the parties are entitled to a properly instructed and informed jury and, if any prejudicial defect is discovered, the entire first trial is tainted incurably.

Another alternative to ordering a new trial is to grant the order conditionally. This typically occurs when the challenge to the first proceeding is that the damages awarded by the jury are either excessive or inadequate as a matter of law. If the court agrees with that assertion, it may try to avoid the cost of a new trial by ruling that it will grant the motion unless the opposing party agrees to a specified reduction or increase in the verdict. Strong arguments against conditional new trial orders have been made on the ground that the judge effectively is supplanting the jury's determination in violation of the parties' rights to a jury decision on the question of damages. By and large these arguments have been unsuccessful. The power to reduce damages (remittitur) is recognized by virtually all judicial systems and has been resistant to constitutional attack. The power to increase damages (additur) does not exist in the federal courts because it has been held to violate the Seventh Amendment. However, additur is allowed in some state courts. The different treatment accorded remittitur and additur in the federal system does not rest on policy, but rather on the fact that remittitur existed at common law and thus is within the scope of the Amendment. Additur is a more modern device and since it does have an impact on the jury's decision, it is not constitutionally permissible. The continued vitality of this distinction is doubted by many today.

There are no specific rules governing the amount to be remitted or added. Different states follow different verbal standards. However, there are three basic formulations that can be identified. The judge may reduce or increase the award to the legally sufficient minimum the jury could have awarded, to the maximum that would have been permissible, or the judge may set the figure between those two extremes at the amount he feels is justified by the evidence. Once the judge applies one of these standards and sets the figure, the opposing party's decision is simply to accept that figure or proceed to a new trial. If the judge's figure is acceptable to the opposing party, the party who originally requested a new trial will find that motion denied and the only option if she is unhappy with the new damage award is to appeal, alleging that even the new figure is improper as a matter of law.

§ 5–16. Combined Motions for New Trial and Judgment Notwithstanding the Verdict

In some judicial systems a party may move simultaneously for a JNOV and for a new trial and the judge must rule on both motions. The theory behind requiring concurrent alternative rulings is that it will save time on appeal and will provide further guidance to the appellate court as to why the judge feels the verdict is erroneous. If the motions were bifurcated with the movant seeking and obtaining first a ruling on the JNOV and then a ruling on new trial, a separate appeal would be required from each of those rulings resulting in a delay of possibly two years or more before a final decision was reached or a new trial actually begun. To avoid this result, the trial judge is instructed to rule on both motions simultaneously.

One effect of the joint rulings is to alter some of the normal appealability rules. As is described elsewhere (see § 7–1, below), most judicial systems authorize appeals only from final judgments. A grant or denial of a JNOV, alone, results in a final judgment being entered. The denial of a new trial motion, alone, also is final as the jury's verdict then is incorporated into a judgment. The grant of a new trial motion is interlocutory, however, as it requires the trial court to begin anew and thus it normally is not immediately appealable. The party must wait to appeal that ruling until after the second trial concludes. As a practical matter, this means that when joint rulings are involved and a new trial is granted, there is no effective appellate review because it will be difficult to show that even if the denial of the JNOV were erroneous, it had a prejudicial effect in the second trial. The rules governing joint JNOV-new trial motions address this problem by providing that if the court grants both the JNOV and the new trial motions, that ruling is appealable immediately. The new trial order is viewed as only an alternative to be used if the JNOV is reversed. If on the initial motion the JNOV is denied and a new trial granted, no immediate appeal lies, however. See Fed.Rule 50(c), (d).

CHAPTER VI

JUDGMENTS AND THEIR EFFECTS

A. RELIEF FROM JUDGMENTS

§ 6–1. Principles Governing

All judicial systems provide some limited means by which a party may seek to set aside a judgment and obtain a new trial after the time for moving for a new trial or appealing has passed. These provisions are attempts to accommodate the need for finality with the desire to make certain that the truth was found in the original trial. Most commonly, relief is allowed only within certain time periods, varying between six months and one year from the entry of the judgment. More rarely, relief is limited only by a reasonable time requirement. Timing restrictions on post judgment relief operate to preserve finality; the certainty produced by finality is merely postponed. The only exception to these rigid time restraints is when the defect in the first proceeding is one going to the very power of the court to try the controversy, as when the court lacked subject-matter or personal jurisdiction.

The most common example of cases in which relief is granted is when there is a default judgment. The due process notion of an effective opportunity to be heard favors adjudications after an adversarial presentation. Thus, the courts treat default relief motions very liberally and will deny relief from those judgments only when it is clear the defendant has no defense to the action or when the defendant has delayed so long that the plaintiff now would be prejudiced by being required to go to trial.

The most common procedure for setting aside a judgment is to make a motion for relief from the judgment under the appropriate rule. It typically is totally within the trial court's discretion whether to grant or deny relief. The court, in addition to considering whether the reasons alleged for setting aside the judgment are permissible grounds for relief under the applicable rule (see § 6–2, below), usually will take into account other equitable concerns. These may include the prejudice to the opposing party, who may have acted in reliance on the judgment, if the motion is granted, whether the movant has proceeded with due diligence in making the motion, or any other matter that might bear on the fairness of reopening the judgment. The court will not consider whether the first judgment is erroneous, although it may take into account whether opening the judgment and ordering a new trial is likely to produce a different result.

Another method by which a party may seek relief is to bring an independent action to set aside the judgment on grounds historically recognized in equity. Additionally, regardless of the specific bases for relief listed in the procedural rules, most systems recognize the right of a party to move to set

aside a judgment for a "fraud on the court." Both
these methods are historically grounded and may
provide an extra safety valve when restrictions in
the rules (usually timing constraints) otherwise
would preclude relief. However, they are encum-
bered with their own historic restrictions, which
most often severely limit their usefulness.

§ 6–2. Grounds for Relief

Federal Rule 60(b) sets out the most widely recognized grounds for seeking relief. Relief may be
granted if the party moves within one year and
shows that the judgment was entered due to a
mistake, surprise, or excusable neglect, or that
some material evidence exists that could not have
been discovered earlier, or that the judgment was
obtained fraudulently. The courts have not interpreted these grounds very broadly. If mistake or
neglect is alleged, gross neglect cannot be found or
relief will be denied. Newly discovered evidence
may be the subject of a motion for relief only if the
evidence was available during the original proceeding. For example, the development of new medical
treatments after a damage verdict has been entered
in a personal injury suit does not qualify as newly
discovered evidence justifying the reopening of the
judgment. The availability of this ground is further
limited because the liberal discovery rules present
in most jurisdictions (see §§ 3–21—3–30, above)
make it most difficult to show that evidence that
existed at the time of the trial could not have been
discovered earlier. In several state systems, a party

moving on the basis of fraud is limited to extrinsic fraud on the theory that the trial itself is designed to weed out intrinsic fraud, such as perjury. In this way the judgment winner is protected from being constantly harassed by relief from judgment motions.

A party also may seek relief on the ground that the judgment is void, that it has been satisfied, or, in the case of an equitable decree, that the circumstances have changed, or that the law on which the court relied has been reversed. In these cases the motion must be made "within a reasonable time." The less rigid time restraints applicable to these bases for relief reflect the seriousness of the defect involved and, in some instances, the fact that it would not be possible to discover the ground until more than one year had passed. It is within the court's discretion to decide whether the motion is so untimely as to prejudice the opposing party unduly. Again, however, the grounds listed are rather specific and are interpreted narrowly.

The last ground for relief also is subject only to the reasonable time limitation; it is the catch-all clause: "any other reason justifying relief." Although its wording is all embrasive, the courts have applied the clause sparingly to only those "extraordinary circumstances" demanding redress. Illustratively, the provision has been invoked successfully when a party has failed to comply with a settlement after a dismissal was entered, and when a party failed to appeal a denaturalization order or move for relief within a year because he was jailed and denied counsel. The courts have not used the clause as a vague loophole to circumvent the other time restrictions.

B. SECURING AND ENFORCING JUDGMENTS

§ 6–3. How a Judgment Is Enforced

Many judgments are self-enforcing. Judgments declaring the law or quieting title are good examples. Other judgments may require the losing party to pay money or to complete some act. In many of these cases a judgment winner need not use any enforcement method because the loser simply will pay the judgment or otherwise comply with the decree. If that does not occur, the method of enforcing the judgment varies depending on whether the judgment is local, that of a sister state, or international in character.

Enforcement of a local judgment is a purely administrative matter. The judgment winner presents a copy of the judgment to the sheriff who issues a writ of execution on property designated by the judgment creditor. The writ orders any person or corporation controlling the property to turn it over to that officer for the purposes of satisfying the judgment winner. Illustratively, the sheriff may issue a writ garnishing the judgment loser's wages until the judgment has been satisfied. A writ of execution also could be directed at the debtor's automobile, which then would be seized and sold at a judicial sale with the proceeds used to pay the judgment. Any excess proceeds would be returned to the judgment loser. In cases in which the judgment is an injunction, the judgment winner can move to hold the loser in contempt of court for failure to comply with the injunction. If so held, the contemnor may be fined or jailed, or both, depending on the court's discretion.

When an out-of-state judgment is involved, it becomes necessary to reduce the judgment to a local one before execution. This requires the judgment creditor to bring an action on the judgment in the local court, serving process on the debtor and providing an opportunity to respond. In virtually all instances a local judgment will be entered with enforcement proceeding as just described. This is because full faith and credit must be given to sister state judgments under the United States Constitution, Article IV, § 1. Therefore, except for a very limited number of objections, the enforcement court cannot look behind the judgment to reexamine the earlier proceedings. The rationale for requiring the creditor to bring an action on the judgment rather than allowing immediate execution is based on notions of sovereignty. Each state is an independent, sovereign power and cannot directly invade another state's authority over its own residents by enforcing a judgment there. Thus, the procedure defers to the sovereignty of the enforcement state by the form of bringing an action asking those courts to recognize the judgment so that execution may follow. International judgments are treated similarly—an action to enforce must be brought. However, there is no constitutional full faith and credit requirement applicable to judgments from a foreign country and the court is given much greater discretion to decide as a matter of comity whether enforcement should take place.

The process of bringing an action on a judgment is often a burdensome formality. Thus, several states have adopted uniform legislation authorizing foreign judgment holders to file the judgment with the local courts and mail a notice to that effect to the judgment debtor. After a short period of time, typically thirty days, in which the debtor can move to vacate, but only on grounds consistent with full faith and credit, the judgment may be executed upon in the same manner as any local court judgment. Uniform Enforcement of Foreign Judgments Act of 1964, 9A Uniform Laws Ann. 488 (1965). The process for enforcing a federal judgment from one state in a federal court in another state is similar, but even simpler. As provided by special statute, 28 U.S.C.A. § 1963, a federal judgment may be registered in another federal court by filing a copy there and, upon that act, it will be treated as a local judgment.

§ 6–4. Securing a Judgment—Constitutional Limitations

In some cases the plaintiff may fear that the defendant will transfer all his property to others or outside of the jurisdiction in order to make the enforcement of any judgment, should he lose, very difficult and costly. In order to secure any possible judgment against this occurring, the plaintiff may request the court to order an attachment or to sequester some of the defendant's assets immediately upon the filing of the action. In this way plaintiff ensures that any judgment obtained will be easily enforceable should defendant refuse to pay.

The process of securing a judgment is governed by state statutes and is accomplished by seeking one of a variety of writs, such as writs of replevin, attachment, garnishment or sequestration. Under most statutes, the plaintiff is required to post a bond, which will be forfeited to the defendant if the suit is found to be frivolous or the attachment solely a means of harassment. The clerk of the court or the judge historically entered the order ex parte and the sheriff seized the property. The defendant received notice only when the seizure took place; he then could appear before the court to ask for relief or to post a counterbond and regain possession of the property.

Prejudgment attachments such as just described have been successfully challenged as violating the constitutional due process rights of the defendant since no hearing or notice is provided prior to the seizure of the property. See Sniadach v. Family Finance Corp. (S.Ct.1969). The Supreme Court in a series of cases in the 1970s evolved a balancing test by which to assess the constitutional validity of any prejudgment attachment statute. See Fuentes v. Shevin (S.Ct.1972). The test takes into account the public or governmental interest that would justify postponing the opportunity to be heard—for example, if attachment depends upon a showing that immediate action is necessary because the defendant is likely to transfer or hide the property. Further, the decision to issue such an order must be committed to the discretion of a judicial officer, not merely the clerk of the court. Finally, the debtor must be provided an opportunity to dissolve the writ immediately, with the burden placed on the plaintiff to show why the attachment was justified. See Mitchell v. W.T. Grant Co. (S.Ct.1974).

Further refinements were added by the Supreme Court in 1991 in Connecticut v. Doehr (S.Ct.1991), when the Court struck down a statutory scheme that allowed the prejudgment attachment of real estate without a showing of extraordinary circumstances and without requiring the plaintiff to post a bond. The Court suggested that the appropriate due process analysis is to weigh the private (defendant's) interests affected by the seizure against the risk of possible erroneous deprivation in light of the procedure involved and the safeguards, such as a bond, that apply, and the need for expeditious handling because of exigent circumstances. Thus, it remains clear that the ability of states to provide prejudgment remedies remains severely limited.

One of the open and important questions raised by this line of cases is to what extent they affect the ability of a court to assert quasi in rem jurisdiction, which necessarily is based on a prejudgment attachment. Is the desire to assert jurisdiction a sufficient governmental interest to justify the delay of the defendant's due process rights to a hearing?

The Supreme Court has not yet ruled on this question and the lower courts that have considered it are divided.

C. THE BINDING EFFECT OF JUDGMENTS

1. IN GENERAL

§ 6–5. The Nomenclature

A complete vocabulary has been developed in connection with the law on the binding effect of judgments. Although the courts sometimes misuse terms, it is important to understand the proper terminology in order to understand the results that may be reached in certain cases.

Res judicata or *claim preclusion* refers to the effect that a final adjudication on the merits of a cause of action (or claim) has on an attempt to relitigate the same cause of action within the same judicial system. It prevents the relitigation of causes of action, regardless of what issues actually were litigated in the first suit. When res judicata is being asserted against a person who was victorious in the first action, the second judgment is said to be merged into the first. *Merger* prevents the second action from going forward. When res judicata is asserted against a person who lost the first suit, the second action is said to be barred by the first. *Bar* prevents the second suit from proceeding. When res judicata is being asserted on the basis of a judgment that was entered in a different court system than the present suit, i.e. another state, or the federal court, if the first action was in the state courts, or vice-versa, the judgment is given binding effect because of *Full Faith and Credit*. The Constitution, Art. IV, § 1, and its enabling legislation, 28 U.S.C.A. § 1738, require the second court to give the first judgment the same effect it would have been given in the forum where it was rendered. Thus, the law of res judicata as developed in the originating court will govern the binding effect of that judgment in the second court. *Collateral estoppel* or *issue preclusion* is invoked when separate causes of action are presented in the first and second suits. The doctrine provides that any issue that was actually and necessarily litigated in one action cannot be relitigated in a subsequent suit.

Claim preclusion and issue preclusion should be distinguished from three other doctrines. *Stare decisis* refers to the policy of the courts to adhere to precedent. Adherence to precedent is the foundation underlying the common law system; it provides the certainty necessary for persons to plan their activities knowing what the governing law is. Stare decisis effect is given only to actual determinations, not dicta. Further, the court has discretion to depart from precedent if it feels the circumstances have changed or that the prior case was decided wrongly. The doctrine of *law of the case* provides that the opinion or judgment of the appellate court on an appeal or writ of error is binding on the trial court when the case is remanded for further action. The doctrine arises out of the rule that a final judgment in the highest court is a final determination of the parties' rights. *Election of remedies* is an historic, common law doctrine developed when parties were not allowed to plead alternatively or inconsistently. It provided that once a party chose between several alternative theories of recovery, he had elected his remedy and, should the action fail, could not then sue on any other theory. A few states still invoke the doctrine to bar inconsistent theories of recovery. Under this approach, for example, to seek reformation, which is premised on the existence of a contract, will preclude a later action for quasi-contract, which assumes no contract exists. However, most courts have abandoned the doctrine.

§ 6–6. General Principles Governing

Res judicata and collateral estoppel both operate with almost total disregard for what the truth is. They are premised on the beliefs that the judicial system cannot tolerate constant relitigation or it will be overburdened; that judgments must be stable and final so that persons will be able to rely on them and plan for the future; and that the judicial system must prevent itself from being used as a tool of harassment. Thus, collateral estoppel precludes the relitigation of the same issues on the assumption that even if the issue was wrongly decided in the first action, the parties had a full and fair opportunity to present their case on that issue and systemic concerns must prevail. Res judicata takes this reasoning one step further. It provides that once the parties have been given a hearing on a claim, there can be no relitigation even though there may be some issues that were never introduced or considered in the first action, but that could have had a substantial impact on the outcome. Both doctrines are extremely important tools for planning litigation as the cautious attorney must take care to frame the case so as not to be precluded in a later action, should a subsequent suit be desirable.

Res judicata and collateral estoppel are judicial doctrines and thus their scope varies from jurisdiction to jurisdiction. Consequently, it is necessary to check in the jurisdiction where suit is brought to determine exactly what binding effect is likely to attach to a particular judgment. There is considerable variation. A general description follows. The reader is advised for more comprehensive treatment to refer to J. Friedenthal, M. Kane & A. Miller, *Civil Procedure* Ch. 14 (2d ed.1993).

2. RES JUDICATA

§ 6–7. Requirements for Asserting

A party asserting res judicata must show that the *same cause of action* or *same claim* is involved in both suits, that there was a *valid* and *final judgment* on that claim, and, in most jurisdictions, that the prior judgment was *on the merits*. The problem of defining what constitutes a single claim or cause of action is discussed in the next section. This section takes a brief look at the other requirements.

The validity of a judgment is determined solely in terms of whether the first court had authority to decide the case, not whether there was error in the first proceeding. Only judgments entered by a court having proper subject-matter jurisdiction (see §§ 2–1—2–6, above), as well as proper personal jurisdiction over the defendant (see §§ 2–9—2–22, above), are entitled to full res judicata effect. However, as was discussed earlier, a judgment may be subject to collateral attack and thus not be given claim preclusive effect because of a lack of jurisdiction only under certain conditions, such as when the defect never was raised in the first proceeding and defendant defaulted there. See § 2–31, above.

Finality, for res judicata purposes, "represents the completion of all steps in the adjudication of a claim by the court, short of execution." American Law Institute, *Restatement Second of Judgments* § 13 (1982). Thus, finality is not affected by the taking of an appeal, unless the appellate court vacates the judgment and orders a trial de novo. Nonetheless, the court in which the judgment is being asserted as binding may stay the action before it until the appeal from the first judgment is prosecuted. While that is the sounder approach because it avoids the risk that binding effect will be given to what ultimately may be found to be an invalid or erroneous judgment, the court has discretion simply to apply res judicata and dismiss the suit based on the first trial court's judgment.

A judgment involving the same cause of action may be final, but still not preclude a second action if it is not on the merits. For example, a dismissal for lack of subject-matter jurisdiction will not bar the identical action from being brought in a court having proper jurisdiction. The requirement of a judgment on the merits has produced some problems with pretrial dismissals that bear closely on the merits. For example, courts do not agree on how to treat demurrers or dismissals for failure to state a claim for relief for res judicata purposes. It is clear that if the pleader merely restates the same complaint in another action, res judicata will apply. Some courts have overruled res judicata challenges when the second complaint alleges other facts or theories, however, concluding that the merits never were actually considered in the first action. Other courts handle this problem by granting the plaintiff a right to amend at the time of the first dismissal. If the plaintiff fails to do so or fails to appeal, then claim preclusion will apply. This approach is particularly prevalent in systems, such as the federal courts, that have very liberal pleading rules and that permit pretrial dismissals on the pleadings only when there is no conceivable theory on which the plaintiff could base the case.

Another problem in determining when a judgment is on the merits is presented by involuntary dismissals entered for failure to prosecute or for failure to comply with some court order. The rules governing these dismissals typically provide that they will be with prejudice unless otherwise ordered. See, e.g., Fed.Rule 41(b). Thus, the question presented is whether they should be given res judicata effect even though it is clear by the very nature of the dismissal that the merits of the case never were reached. The weight of authority applies res judicata, noting that the availability of motions for relief from judgment and of an appeal ameliorates the harshness of this decision. Other courts refuse preclusive effect on the ground that the dismissal is not on the merits.

In order to avoid the kinds of problems just discussed, the American Law Institute, *Restatement Second of Judgments* § 19, Comment a (1982), omits entirely the phrase "on the merits" from its definition of bar. Instead, the question whether preclusive effect should be given to a pretrial dismissal is determined as a matter of sound judicial administration and by considering the fairness to the defendant if a second action is allowed. Both of these concerns require that the litigation terminate once and for all after the first dismissal and the question whether the court's decision involved the merits is irrelevant.

§ 6–8. Defining a Cause of Action or Claim

The particular test that a court adopts defining cause of action (or claim) may be influenced by several outside considerations. Some courts utilize a very broad test in keeping with the policies of their judicial systems to encourage the broadest possible joinder of claims and defenses in the first suit and thereby avoid multiple suits. Others invoke a more narrow conception because they are concerned about the harsh effect of claim preclusion and prefer to rely on collateral estoppel to prevent duplicative litigation. Yet others may be influenced by the merits of the claim of the party opposing the assertion of res judicata and thus define the cause of action most narrowly to allow the presentation of the case. A few courts appear to take into account whether the cause of action was split intentionally. What follows is a description of the various tests utilized by different courts. However, whichever test is used in the forum court, the court also may be swayed in applying its standards by the factors just mentioned.

There are essentially four different tests that have been used to define what constitutes a cause of action. The first, which may be called the *destruction-of-prior-judgment* test, focusses on the question whether a decision in the second action would have the effect of undoing or contradicting what is embraced in the first judgment. This test can be applied in different ways depending on what the court considers as being within the scope of the first judgment. Thus, res judicata may be invoked successfully under this standard if the court considers the judgment to include not only the relief awarded but all the explicit and implicit findings that supported that award of relief; if the court focusses merely on the desire to avoid providing an inconsistent remedy, then the test is very narrow indeed and no preclusive effect will be given.

A second conception of cause of action looks to the legal rights and wrongs involved in the first suit and seeks to prevent multiple lawsuits based on grounds for the same wrong or injury. This is sometimes referred to as the *primary rights* test. Under it, separate causes of action are involved when more than one right was infringed, even though the several rights involved were impinged upon by a single act. For example, personal injury and car damages arising from the same accident present different causes of action under this standard because one involves trespass to the person, the other trespass to a chattel. However, back injuries and neurological damage constitute the violation of one right—trespass to person. Actions involving separate pieces of property also involve different rights. Res judicata will be applied in contract disputes depending on whether the contract is deemed indivisible or divisible, providing for separate rights. In a somewhat similar vein, if the legal rights in two actions rest on different statutes, then multiple causes of action will be found.

The "primary rights" definition of cause of action is a product of the common law writ system when cases could consist only of a single issue and thus most courts do not adhere to it today. Although it was necessary then to protect parties from preclusion because they could not have raised multiple causes in one suit, modern claim joinder affords that opportunity and suggests that a broader res judicata test be utilized. See § 3–19, above. In order to modernize the test, a variant has evolved in some states that defines rights, not in terms of historic distinctions, but in terms of the wrongs that were committed. Thus, focus under this approach is on the defendant's acts, rather than the plaintiff's injuries. One tortious act constitutes one cause of action even though it may have produced a series of injuries to person and property. In actions based on violations of property or contract rights, the focus will be on the acts of the defendant that produced injury or served to breach.

The third approach to defining cause of action attempts to avoid duplicative litigation by determining whether the *same evidence* would be used in both actions. The difficulty with this standard—and the probable reason why it has not gained wide acceptance—is that there is no sure measuring rod as to how much evidence should be the same before it is proper to find that the same cause of action is presented.

The fourth and broadest test for the assertion of res judicata is the *transaction* test, proposed in American Law Institute, *Restatement Second of Judgments* § 24(1) (1982). Under that standard any acts or series of occurrences that may have produced an injury or series of injuries should be presented in a single suit. The obvious effect of this approach is to create compulsory joinder of claims in the first action. Thus, there has been some resistance to the transaction standard on the ground that if the pleading and joinder rules are permissive only (see § 3–19, above), then it is unfair and improper for the courts to create a compulsory joinder system indirectly through the application of res judicata. However, as more and more judicial systems have adopted procedural rules encouraging the broadest possible joinder of claims, the application of the transaction test to determine what claims might have to be presented in a single proceeding has received growing acceptance.

The application of the various standards just described to the assertion of claims in a second action by the person who was the defendant in the first suit must be considered separately. Both the "rights" and the "wrong" test for cause of action necessitate not only that the same parties or their privies be involved in both suits, see § 6–9, below, but also that the parties remain in essentially the same offensive-defensive posture in both actions. In an action between A and B, those tests look to how many of A's rights were violated or how many wrongful acts were committed by B. If B also has a potential claim against A arising out of the same series of events, that will constitute a separate cause of action because it will require an inquiry into B's rights and A's wrongful acts. The transaction test does not recognize this distinction and res judicata could apply to both A's and B's claims under the transaction standard.

Defining cause of action in terms of whose rights or wrongs are involved has caused some problems in situations in which the same facts may be asserted by B as an affirmative defense or as a counterclaim. The judicial economy and harassment rationales underlying the doctrine of claim preclusion suggest that B should be compelled to raise both the defense and the counterclaim in the first suit. Although this result may be readily achieved in jurisdictions that have a compulsory counterclaim rule, (see § 3–20, above), in states without such a provision the result rests on the application of res judicata principles. Indeed, a broad application of those principles might suggest that even if B defaults res judicata should bar another action by B against A, because B had the opportunity to raise the defense, and the counterclaim was merged into the defense.

Most courts faced with this problem have not gone so far. A distinction is drawn between omitted and litigated defenses, with res judicata being applied in a subsequent suit by B against A only if B asserted the affirmative defense, but failed to include the counterclaim. The focus in determining whether B has split the cause of action is whether the same facts are in issue and the same evidence will be utilized for both the defense and the omitted claim. Some courts have refused to go even that far. They have applied the same evidence test in such a way that res judicata cannot ever be invoked successfully in this situation by pointing to new evidence on damages, not germane to the defense, to substantiate the conclusion that there are different causes of action.

§ 6–9. Who Will Be Bound

The doctrine of res judicata is applicable only when the second action is between persons who were parties or who are in privity with persons who were parties in the first action. When new parties are involved in the second action, a separate or different cause of action is presented. If any preclusive effect is to attach to the first judgment, it will be through the application of collateral estoppel, not res judicata. See § 6–13, below. The sole exception to this is when a class action judgment is involved—all absent class members will be bound by that judgment. (See § 8–4, below.) Thus, the question of who will be bound by res judicata depends upon the definition of who is in privity with the named parties in the first action.

Historically, a person in privity with a party was one who acquired an interest in the subject matter of the suit after it had been brought. Successors in interest, whether they obtained their interests by virtue of an assignment, by inheritance or by law were treated as parties for res judicata purposes and were bound by any judgment entered against or for their predecessors. Modern courts have extended privity concepts to additional circumstances. For example, a person who actually controls the first suit will be found to be in privity with the named parties to that suit. Appointed or legal representatives, such as guardians or administrators, are in privity with the person whom they are representing. Additionally, privity has been found in a wide range of commercial relationships, such as those involving employer-employee and indemnitor-indemnitee relationships. The decision to expand privity to those relationships depends heavily on the substantive law regulating the relationship and generalizations about the binding effect of judgments in those areas are dangerous because of the complicated nature of the rules used to determine both who can claim privity, as well as when privity is appropriate.

Suffice it to note here that the modern trend has been to expand the scope of res judicata to bind persons whose interests are so tied to those of existing parties that it would be a waste of judicial effort to allow a second action to go forward simply because they were not named in the first suit. However, because claim preclusion effects are so drastic—precluding issues that ought to have been litigated, as well as those that actually were litigated—courts still refuse to extend privity to embrace persons having similar, or even identical, interests if there is no special relationship existing between those individuals. Thus, for example, the fact that the same lawyer is representing the parties in the first and second action will not, standing alone, establish privity. The focus is on the type of relationship between the party and the alleged privy, as well as whether they share an identity of interest in light of that relationship.

§ 6–10. Policies Outweighing Res Judicata

There are some circumstances in which even though the standard for applying res judicata has been met, preclusion will not result. These situations arise when the judicial economy policies fostered by claim preclusion are outweighed by some other public policy underlying the type of action that is involved. Illustratively, in a suit involving the sale of land in which both the buyer and the seller were seeking title, a court overruled all res judicata objections because to hold otherwise would be inequitable and would result in unclear title to the land.   The policies underlying the transfer of property required that some determination regarding ownership be given the parties.   Adams v. Pearson (Ill.1952).   In another action res judicata was outweighed by the policies underlying the worker's compensation laws so that a prior common law negligence action did not preclude the statutory remedy, it only reduced the amount of the judgment therein.   Varsity Amusement Co. v. Butters (Colo. 1964).   Necessarily, these exceptions to the normal application of claim preclusion principles are limited.   They depend on a finding of specific and important social policies requiring the abandonment of res judicata.

3.   COLLATERAL ESTOPPEL

§ 6–11.   Requirements for Asserting

In order for collateral estoppel to be invoked successfully, the party asserting estoppel must show that the same or *identical issue* is presented in action–2 that was decided in action–1, and that the issue was *actually* and *necessarily* decided in the action–1.   The presence of each element of this test assures that preclusion will result only after a party has had a full opportunity to litigate the particular issue.   Conversely, judicial economy becomes paramount when this assurance exists.

The requirement of identical issues is met easily when the plaintiff is asserting several claims based on a single wrongful act of the defendant. The question whether the defendant acted negligently in driving an automobile will be the same in a suit claiming damages for personal injuries to the driver of the other car as in a later suit by the driver's spouse for loss of consortium. However, in actions arising out of acts that occurred at different times, the issues, though similar, necessarily are not identical. For example, a suit in 1987 to establish the taxability of income made by an organization claiming a tax exemption as a religious group will have no preclusive effect on a similar action in 1988. A finding that the defendant did or did not function as a religious organization in 1987 will not be given issue preclusive effect because the character of the defendant's activities in 1988 may have changed— the issue is not identical. Similarly, collateral estoppel will not be available in successive actions on separate bonds or negotiable instruments in which the same defense—whether the plaintiff purchased the bonds for value—is raised. The issues are not identical; the proof that the plaintiff was or was not a bona fide purchaser of one bond, does not serve to prove how any of the other bonds were obtained.

Differences in the burden of proof in the first and second action also may result in a finding that the issues presented in both suits are not identical. This restriction recognizes that if the burden of proof differs, there is no assurance that the result would be the same in both actions and the requirements of collateral estoppel are designed to provide that assurance. The issue arises most often when one proceeding is criminal and the other civil, because in criminal suits the prosecution must prove each element beyond a reasonable doubt, but in civil actions the plaintiff need only establish the claim by a preponderance of the evidence. If an issue is established first under the stricter standard, then it may be given collateral estoppel effect in the later civil proceeding, but the converse is not true.

The requirement that the issues actually be litigated prevents collateral estoppel effect from being given to default judgments or consent judgments in which a determination on the merits is reached, but a full adversary presentation on the underlying issues has not occurred. The requirement is more difficult to apply, however, in cases in which a review of the pleadings fails to reveal whether the issues framed there actually were litigated at the trial and thus are embraced by the judgment. This problem occurs, for example, when a general verdict is rendered and the judgment could be based on findings on one or more issues in the case. The minority view is that the court in the second action is to treat all issues as actually litigated, giving a very broad collateral estoppel effect to the judgment. The majority view is that when the judgment in the first action may have been based on findings on more than one issue, no collateral estoppel effect will be given to any issue in the case unless evidence is introduced showing which issues actually were decided. As a further limitation, only extrinsic evidence that supports the verdict is allowed; the evidence cannot contradict the verdict. For example, consider an action in which A sues B for injuries caused by B's negligence. B alleges as a defense that A was contributorily negligent. There is a general verdict for B. That verdict could be based on a finding that A was contributorily negligent, that B was free from negligence, or both. B can assert collateral estoppel in a subsequent suit against A only if B can show on what the jury rested its verdict. However, under no circumstances can A introduce evidence to the effect that his alleged contributory negligence was not actually litigated or considered by the jury because that would contradict the verdict.

The third requirement for asserting collateral estoppel—whether the issue was necessary to the first proceeding—has posed great difficulty for the courts. This requirement assures that the parties vigorously litigated the issue so that it is fair to prevent its relitigation in a second action because there is little likelihood that the results will be different the second time around. The courts have developed a few general rules to aid in this inquiry. Facts found against the prevailing party in the first action are deemed unnecessary. The prevailing party has no incentive to appeal and thus the issue will not be given collateral estoppel effect because vigorous prosecution on that issue is not assured. On the other hand, alternative holdings are given full collateral estoppel effect; there is no need to determine which finding was necessary to the judgment. It is assumed that one issue is no less necessary than the other. For example, in the negligence hypothetical above, if a special verdict had been rendered specifically finding A contributorily negligent and B free from negligence, B could assert collateral estoppel against A on both those issues. Interestingly, the American Law Institute, *Restatement Second of Judgments* § 27 (1982), advocates that no collateral estoppel effect be given in this situation because of a concern that this broad approach will encourage appeals. However, if the parties have appealed and the appellate court affirms the alternative findings, then the Restatement would apply collateral estoppel to those issues.

§ 6–12. Mediate and Ultimate Facts

Another method utilized by the courts to determine when to uphold the assertion of collateral estoppel was to distinguish between mediate and ultimate facts, giving preclusive effect only to the latter. Ultimate facts were those on which the case was based—e.g., does plaintiff have title. Mediate facts were those that provided the means by which the court could reach a conclusion on the ultimate facts—e.g., did plaintiff obtain title through a fraudulent scheme. Concerns over how to prove whether a mediate fact actually was litigated led to a rule that mediate facts in the first action would not be given collateral estoppel effect. Another concern prompting the use of the mediate/ultimate fact distinction was the problem of foreseeability. This concern was particularly prevalent when a fact found in the first action, whether mediate or ultimate there, was only a mediate fact in the second action.   Courts refused collateral estoppel effect under those circumstances in order to prevent surprise to the losing litigant who, it was assumed, could not have foreseen all the possible future mediate facts that might be associated with a given issue and thus may not have litigated the issue fully the first time.

The mediate/ultimate fact distinction is largely of historic significance.   The policies it addressed are satisfied in other ways without relying on pleading distinctions that have lost much of their meaning.   Further, the availability of devices such as special verdicts and general verdicts with interrogatories has eroded the need for this rule.   See § 5–10, above.   The American Law Institute, *Restatement Second of Judgments* § 27 (1982), states that the modern approach is to determine whether the fact issue on which collateral estoppel is being asserted was necessary and important, rather than merely evidentiary, in the first suit.   If so and the issue was actually litigated, then it is fair to give the issue preclusive effect in another action.   There is no need to be concerned with foreseeability because the parties had incentive to vigorously litigate the issue in the first proceeding.

§ 6–13. Who Will Be Bound

Historically, the question of who could benefit from or who would be bound by collateral estoppel was treated the same way as when res judicata was involved: only parties and their privies could invoke or be precluded by estoppel. See § 6–9, above. Even though an issue was identical in two different actions and judicial economy concerns would support preventing its relitigation in a second action, collateral estoppel effect was denied. The reasoning supporting this restriction was twofold. In cases in which collateral estoppel is asserted against someone who was not a party to the first action, due process prevents its application because the non-party must be given an opportunity to be heard. The doctrine of mutuality prevented the successful assertion of collateral estoppel by a non-party against someone who did litigate the first suit. That doctrine is premised on the notion that everyone should be treated equally. Since a party to an action cannot assert collateral estoppel against someone who was not a party to that suit, neither should the non-party be allowed to assert estoppel against the party. In this way mutuality operated in favor of someone who had been heard, giving that person a second chance to prove the issue.

Although due process continues to prevent the assertion of collateral estoppel against one who was not a party to the first suit, the question whether mutuality is a necessary limitation on the scope of collateral estoppel is debatable. Thus, perhaps not surprisingly, adherence to the doctrine of mutuality has been steadily eroding, following the lead of California in Bernhard v. Bank of America Nat. Trust & Sav. Ass'n (Cal.1942). Those courts who have abandoned the doctrine have concluded that a person should not be allowed to continuously litigate a fruitless claim, particularly when relitigation is unlikely to change the result. Instead of automatically denying preclusive effect to a non-party asserting estoppel against a party, they focus on whether the party had a full and fair opportunity to litigate the issue in the first action. If so, then collateral estoppel may be applied. Of course, the issues must be identical in both suits.

Courts have abandoned mutuality in varying degrees. The most commonly recognized situation is when the person asserting issue preclusion is doing so defensively. In those cases judicial economy concerns are great because it appears that the party to the first suit simply may be suing seriatim. There is a desire to protect the new defendant from such harassing litigation. The problem becomes more difficult when collateral estoppel is being asserted offensively—when a non-party is attempting to take advantage of a judgment that is adverse to a party in the first suit. Certainly, there is less need to be concerned about the new party, and there is a much greater concern about the defendant. Did the defendant foresee this second suit at the time of the first action so that he had the incentive to litigate that suit fully? Some courts have refused to allow collateral estoppel to be asserted offensively by a non-party. Others have allowed its assertion when it is against someone who was the aggressor in the first suit, but not when it is against someone who was a defendant in the first suit. This distinction is based on the belief that the defending party to the first action necessarily was at a disadvantage in that suit and to make certain that the party has a fair opportunity to be heard, collateral estoppel should not be applied. A few courts have refused to reject collateral estoppel merely because of the posture of the parties. Instead, they focus on whether the party to both actions could have foreseen the second suit. If so, the burden shifts to that party to show that the issue was not fully litigated in the first action. If that is not shown, collateral estoppel will be applied.

The United States Supreme Court has endorsed the abandonment of mutuality in the federal courts and has set out guidelines for those courts to aid in evaluating the propriety of the assertion of collateral estoppel by non-parties. Parklane Hosiery Co. v. Shore (S.Ct.1979). The Court ruled that the trial court has broad discretion to determine this question and that collateral estoppel should be applied even when it is being asserted by a plaintiff against someone who was a defendant in the first action unless the court finds that the plaintiff easily could have joined in the first action or that its application of collateral estoppel would be unfair to the defendant. The federal standard thus looks not only to foreseeability, but also to other potential unfairness, and it seeks to avoid rewarding a plaintiff who chooses not to join in the first suit in order not to be bound by that judgment, if it were in favor of the defendant. Fairness also may take into account whether there is any reason to fear that the judgment is aberrational and whether there are procedural opportunities available in the second action that did not exist in the first, suggesting that a different result might be obtained if the issue were retried. (However, the Parklane Court specifically held that the availability of a jury trial in the second suit is not such an opportunity.)

The state courts are not obliged to follow the lead of the Supreme Court and many continue to define categories of cases in which mutuality applies. Thus, it is most important to check the law of the judgment rendering court to determine who may use collateral estoppel because variations between jurisdictions in their adherence to mutuality are great.

§ 6–14. Limitations on Collateral Estoppel

The availability of collateral estoppel may be limited by other policies outweighing the desire for judicial economy and certainty. For example, it was argued that the doctrine could not be invoked when to do so would effectively deny the opposing party a right to a jury trial on an issue because the first suit was tried without a jury. The Supreme Court rejected this argument, however, ruling that an equitable determination can have issue preclusive effect in a subsequent legal action without violating the Seventh Amendment. Parklane Hosiery Co. v. Shore (S.Ct.1979).

A limitation on the application of collateral estoppel that does arise is when the first action was before a court of limited jurisdiction. The courts are divided on the question whether to give collateral estoppel effect to issues when the claims raised in the second action to which those issues pertain were outside the jurisdictional power of the first court. The question becomes even more acute when the second court has exclusive jurisdiction over the claims before it. This question has arisen in antitrust and patent cases in the federal courts when there have been prior state proceedings in which those courts have ruled on issues pertaining to antitrust violations or patent validity in the course of deciding whether a contract was illegal or whether royalties were due under a licensing agreement. An early decision by the Second Circuit held that the punitive and exclusive nature of the federal antitrust remedy precludes collateral estoppel in that setting. Lyons v. Westinghouse Elec. Corp. (2d Cir.1955). However, estoppel may be applied to some of the underlying facts. Thus, the Supreme Court recognized in a patent case that issue preclusion was proper as to any of the underlying facts; the courts might refrain from giving collateral estoppel only to the "congerie of facts" establishing the ultimate issue of patent validity or infringement. Becher v. Contoure Laboratories, Inc. (S.Ct. 1929). In this way the federal courts avoid duplicative relitigation, but protect their exclusive right to rule on the patent itself. More recently, however, even this distinction appears to be losing its vitality and federal courts increasingly are finding that the notion of federal exclusive jurisdiction does not pose an absolute barrier to collateral estoppel. Thus, collateral estoppel may be disallowed when the original court was a court of limited jurisdiction only if the limitations on that court suggest some serious differences in the quality and existence of procedures available there. For example, judgments of small claims courts typically are given no issue preclusive effect.

The final limitation on the application of collateral estoppel arises because of changes in the law that occur between the first and second lawsuits. If the law is altered to change the operative facts necessary to obtain a favorable ruling, then collateral estoppel will not apply. To hold otherwise would result in unequal treatment being afforded persons under the law simply because of the fortuity of a person obtaining a prior ruling. For example, A brings a tax refund action on the theory that an assignment of royalties under a 1928 patent licensing agreement to his wife B was valid so that income under that agreement during the years 1929–1931 was not taxable to him. The court finds the assignment valid and thus A is not liable for tax on those royalties, but is due a refund. The law changes as to what must be shown to constitute a valid assignment between husband and wife. Collateral estoppel will not be available to A in a refund suit for taxes collected on royalties earned from 1937–41 on the issue of whether there has been a valid assignment; new additional evidence must be introduced. Commissioner v. Sunnen (S.Ct.1948). The need for tax equality outweighs the judicial economy policies underlying collateral estoppel.

It is worth noting that concern over changes in law led some courts to suggest that issue preclusion never is appropriate for issues of pure law. Consequently, several decisions can be found in which the courts have struggled to determine what constitutes an issue of law rather than one of fact or one of mixed fact and law, to which estoppel can be applied. More modern courts have abandoned this approach, however, instead focussing on whether changes in the law suggest that estoppel would be inappropriate.

CHAPTER VII

APPEALS

A. TIME FOR BRINGING AN APPEAL

1. THE FINAL JUDGMENT RULE

§ 7–1. Final Judgment Rule

Most jurisdictions authorize an appeal only from the entry of a final judgment in the action. The final judgment is defined as that order that leaves nothing to be done in the action except to execute on the judgment. It concludes all the rights that were subject to litigation. For example, an order dismissing a juror for cause, though conclusive on that question, is not a final judgment because the rights that are the subject of the underlying lawsuit have not been decided. If the attorney objects to the ruling, that objection may be raised on appeal, but the attorney must wait to take an appeal until a judgment is entered. This type of order commonly is described as reviewable, but not appealable. The only exceptions to the final judgment rule are incorporated in specific statutes, see § 7–3, below, or in a few well-recognized judicial doctrines, see § 7–4, below.

The rationale supporting the final judgment rule are severalfold. In part the rule stems from a desire to obtain judicial economy—a single appeal in which all objections to the trial court's rulings are raised should be more efficient than several appeals, each requiring its own set of briefs, records, oral argument, and opinions. Indeed, the need for an appeal on a given ruling may be avoided totally if the losing party on that issue ultimately prevails in the trial court. Appeals from final judgments also avoid the problem of delaying the trial in order to decide interlocutory matters. This further protects against the possibility that an appeal may be used to harass the opposing party.

A few jurisdictions, such as New York, have not been persuaded by these arguments and are very permissive about allowing immediate appeals from trial court orders. These jurisdictions focus on the fact that an immediate appeal may avoid an unnecessary trial if the question is one that will decide whether the suit should proceed. Alternatively, an immediate appeal may result in a better trial as all preliminary issues will be resolved fully. Further, the final judgment rule effectively prevents some orders from ever being reviewed because they do not affect the merits and will not be deemed sufficiently prejudicial to merit review after the trial is completed. The absence of appellate guidance on these matters can result in inconsistent treatment by the lower courts. Allowing interlocutory appeals on all preliminary orders assures the appellate courts the opportunity to fulfill their function of establishing uniform law.

Thus, there are persuasive arguments supporting and criticizing the final judgment rule. The important thing to note is whether the jurisdiction in which suit is filed adheres to the rule. In addition, differences exist between jurisdictions following the rule in interpreting what is "final" and in the exceptions that are recognized. The question of what constitutes finality is one which has posed significant difficulties for the courts. Thus, it is most critical to consult the law in the jurisdiction where the initial proceeding is filed to determine whether an immediate appeal is allowed because the failure to take an immediate appeal, if it is permitted, will waive the right to raise that issue on an appeal from the final judgment.

§ 7–2. Specialized Rules for Multi–Claim, Multi–Party Cases

The application of the final judgment rule in multi-claim, multi-party litigation has posed some problems when the trial court reaches a final decision on some of the claims before it is ready to render judgment on the entire action. Postponing an appeal until all the claims have been decided may result in an unnecessary delay on a claim that has been fully and finally determined. Thus, special rules have been developed for identifying those orders in multi-claim, multi-party disputes that determine finally the action as it pertains to a given party or claim in order to allow an immediate appeal in those situations. These provisions are not exceptions to the final judgment rule. Rather, they represent standards for applying that rule in those contexts.

A good example is Federal Rule 54(b). Under that rule, in an action having multiple claims or parties, the trial court identifies its order as appealable by making an express direction for the entry of a judgment on the claim involved and by certifying that there is no just reason to delay the appeal. In the absence of this two-part certification, the appellate court will dismiss the appeal as violative of the final judgment rule. If the certification is present, the appellate court will review the decision of the trial court that there was no just reason to delay the appeal, utilizing an abuse of discretion standard. It will consider de novo whether in fact more than one claim is present in the suit or whether the court merely ruled on one of the alternative theories on which the plaintiff's single claim was based and whether a final determination has been made on that claim.

Both of these criteria have caused some difficulties for the trial and appellate courts. When multiple parties are present multiple claims may be easily identified, but certification is proper only if all the claims relating to one of the parties have been determined. In two-party disputes the standard exercised is that multiple claims are present if the theories of recovery that are presented could have been separately and concurrently enforced; the fact that the claims are related or rest on overlapping facts does not prevent a finding that multiple claims exist. As to the second determination, in general, courts are agreed that only the infrequent, harsh case merits a finding that there is no just reason for delay. The court must balance whether the appeal could simplify the trial or whether it would result in a repetitive review of many of the same issues after a judgment is reached on the remaining claims. Similarly, it may weigh the immediate benefit of a recovery to the winning party on an earlier appeal against the possibility that the judgment on one claim should be stayed because it may be set-off by a judgment for the opposing party on the remaining claims.

2. EXCEPTIONS TO THE FINAL JUDGMENT RULE

§ 7–3. Statutory Interlocutory Appeals Routes

A brief examination of the federal interlocutory appeals statutes provides a good illustration of the types of exceptions that typically are recognized in systems observing the final judgment rule. For a more extended discussion, see C. Wright, *Law of Federal Courts* 749–58 (5th ed.1994).

In one statute, 28 U.S.C.A. § 1292(b), a general procedure for discretionary interlocutory appeals is provided requiring the trial court and the appellate court both to certify that the order should be appealed immediately. The standard for certification is that the issue involves a "controlling question of law," that there is "substantial ground for difference of opinion" on that issue, and that an immediate appeal may "materially advance the ultimate termination of the litigation." The purpose of this appeals route is to allow immediate review of important questions. By requiring certification at both levels, the trial court, which is most familiar with the entire proceeding, can rule on whether the appellant raises a crucial issue or is appealing as a dilatory tactic. The appellate court can estimate better its own burdens and can make its decision on appealability relatively free from pressures by the litigants. The standard rests heavily on the discretion of both courts and there may be considerable differences of opinion as to whether any given issue is controlling or as to what will aid the early termination of the suit.

The other statutory appeals measure is embodied in 28 U.S.C.A. § 1292(a). That provision sets out specific categories of orders or types of proceedings from which an interlocutory appeal is permissible. It lists four categories: (1) orders "granting, continuing, modifying, refusing or dissolving injunctions, or refusing to dissolve or modify injunctions"; (2) orders involving receiverships; (3) interlocutory decrees in admiralty cases; and (4) judgments in patent infringement suits that are final except for an accounting. Each one of these exceptions is quite concrete and represents a decision based on concerns that in these areas immediacy is terribly important. Analogous state provisions delineate other orders that are perceived as demanding immediate appellate review. For example, Minnesota includes a right of appeal to the state Supreme

Court from an order vacating or sustaining an attachment. Minn.R.Civ.App. § 103.03(c). Other states specifically authorize appeals from orders granting new trial motions. Cal.Civ.Proc.Code § 904.1(a)(4).

§ 7–4. Judicial Interlocutory Appeals Routes

There are a few well-recognized judicial exceptions to the final judgment rule by which the courts will allow an appeal even though portions of the case remain undecided. The most famous of these is the *collateral order doctrine*. Under the collateral order doctrine an immediate appeal may be taken from an order that is final and unrelated to the merits (collateral) but that, if it is not appealed immediately, may result in irreparable harm to the appellant. Cohen v. Beneficial Industrial Loan Corp. (S.Ct.1949). The appellate court determines whether this standard has been met when the appeal is filed.

Determining whether an order is collateral has not posed too much difficulty for the courts. Many orders are clearly unrelated to the merits. Those that are separate, but more closely intertwined, also may meet the standard. However, in those cases the courts place much greater emphasis on the irreparable harm portion of the standard. What constitutes irreparable harm is within the court's discretion. In large measure the court will focus on the severity of the potential injury, the probability of harm occurring, and the likelihood that review would be ineffective if it were delayed. Examples of some orders that have been held within the collateral order doctrine are: the denial of a motion to impose security for costs on plaintiffs in a shareholder derivative suit; the denial of a motion to proceed in forma pauperis; and the grant of a motion to require the plaintiff in a class action to send individual notice to all the unnamed class members.

In the federal class action area an off-shoot of the collateral order doctrine was developed termed the *death knell doctrine*. Orders denying class certification are not truly collateral because the certification process often requires some inquiry into the merits of the underlying claims, if only to examine what common questions are involved. Also, they are not final since the court is directed to consider their revision throughout the trial. However, in many class suits the individual members each have only very small claims and it would not be feasible to bring the action except as a class suit, so that denial of class certification may result as a practical matter in ending the litigation. In response to this possibility, the Second Circuit developed the death knell doctrine, allowing an immediate appeal under these circumstances on the theory that the refusal to certify the class was effectively a final order collateral to the merits that if not appealable would result in the death of the action, irreparably harming the plaintiffs. Eisen v. Carlisle & Jacquelin (2d Cir.1966). An appeal also was authorized from an order granting class certification on what was termed an "inverse death knell theory." Herbst v.

International Tel. & Tel. Corp. (2d Cir.1974). The Supreme Court ultimately rejected the death knell doctrine (and by implication the inverse death knell doctrine). It ruled that the doctrine violated the final judgment rule and insofar as it rested on the peculiar nature of class actions, the decision whether to allow an appeal should be a legislative one. Coopers & Lybrand v. Livesay (S.Ct.1978).

Another judicial interlocutory appeals route authorizes the appellate court to allow an appeal from a nonfinal decision having *irremediable consequences*. The device was first invoked by the Supreme Court in Forgay v. Conrad (S.Ct.1848). In that case, the district court made a partial adjudication of a claim, but ordered the losing party to deliver the physical property involved to the opponent immediately. In that way it treated its partial ruling as final. The appellate court allowed the appeal to avoid the potentially irreparable harm that would occur to the losing party in the absence of immediate review. The courts have used this irremediable consequences rationale very seldom, but it does represent an exception created to provide justice when the application of the final judgment rule would operate very harshly.

§ 7–5. Extraordinary Routes of Appeal

There are two extraordinary routes of appeal that must be mentioned, though they are of limited use. The first is an application to the appellate court for a *writ of mandamus* ordering the trial court to reverse its ruling. Mandamus is based on the theory that the trial court has abused its discretion to such a degree that the appellate court must consider the question immediately. It typically can be used successfully only in extreme cases because it represents a deliberate and direct interference with the lower court during the course of a trial. For example, mandamus was held proper when the appellate court found that the judge had totally abdicated his judicial function by essentially allowing a case to be tried by a master. La Buy v. Howes Leather Co. (S.Ct.1957). It also was used to review Judge Sirica's ruling on the discoverability of the presidential tapes because of the public interest in ending the controversy over that issue as soon as possible. Nixon v. Sirica (D.C.Cir.1973).

Although mandamus typically is utilized only in extraordinary circumstances, a few states have made greater use of that appeals route to provide for immediate review of certain issues. Illustratively, in California rulings denying motions to quash service of process on the ground of lack of personal jurisdiction must be appealed immediately by an application for mandamus. Cal.Civ.Proc.Code § 418.10. This use of mandamus is so deeply rooted that failure to so act results in a waiver of the objection; personal jurisdiction cannot be raised on a later appeal from the final judgment.

Another extraordinary route of appeal that should be noted is *contempt*. This method most commonly is available when discovery orders are involved. Failure to obey the court's order will result in the disobedient party being held in contempt. A contempt judgment is a final judgment and may be appealed immediately. This method of appeal necessarily is very risky since if the appellate court affirms the lower court's discovery order, the contempt judgment will stand. Further, only criminal contempt is immediately appealable so that if the court determines that the party was adjudged in civil contempt, an appeal may not be allowed and the contempt judgment will remain. The difference between civil and criminal contempt is discussed elsewhere. Suffice it to say it depends on the nature of the proceeding and the type of sentence imposed. See D. Dobbs, *Remedies* 138–145 (2d ed.1993). Despite these risks, in some cases this method has been utilized to avoid the delay that would result in adhering to the final judgment rule in the main action.

B. THE MECHANICS OF APPEAL

§ 7–6. Appealable Issues

While it might seem obvious that the losing party can appeal adverse findings, the rules concerning what issues can be raised on appeal or cross-appeal are somewhat more complex. To begin with, only rulings that were objected to in the trial court may be presented by the appellant. Losing parties may appeal all adverse rulings to which they objected. However, winning parties may not appeal from findings deemed erroneous if those findings are not necessary to the decree. The rationale for this restriction is that unnecessary findings will not be the basis for collateral estoppel (see § 6–11, above), and thus there is no need for the appeal because no prejudice will result to the winning party by denying it.

On the other hand, if the losing party appeals, the appellee may raise in response any issue that would sustain the judgment, whether or not it was decided below. The basic question in deciding whether the appellee can raise new grounds sustaining the judgment is one of fairness: is the case in the same basic posture it would have been had the issue been introduced below.

The appellee also is limited to raising issues in support of the judgment, unless he files a cross-appeal. This is particularly important in the third-party context. Assume A sues B for personal injuries and B joins C, the insurer, as a third-party defendant based on an indemnity theory. A loses and the claim against C is dismissed as no right to indemnity arose. A appeals. If B wants to preserve the right to indemnity in the event of a reversal, B must cross-appeal against C, B cannot merely raise that issue by way of responsive brief.

§ 7–7. Standard of Review

The scope and standard of review that will be used by the appellate court will depend on the nature of the alleged error—whether it involved an issue of fact or one of law—as well as whether the trial was before a jury or not. The fullest scope of review is for errors of law: appellate courts may decide such questions de novo. Rulings that are committed to the trial judge's discretion are reviewed under an abuse of discretion standard, however, which allows reversal only if the trial judge was clearly wrong.

Findings of fact receive greater deference than issues of law. In a case tried to a judge, they may be overturned only if they are clearly erroneous. See Fed.Rule 52(a). This means that only if the trial judge's findings are based on a misunderstanding of the law or are totally without evidentiary support will they be reversed. Mixed questions of fact and law are treated as pure questions of law and are subject to full review. When a jury trial is involved, the appellate court will give even greater deference to the findings because constitutional jury trial rights typically protect the jurors' factual determinations from review except to the extent allowed at Common Law.

CHAPTER VIII

SPECIALIZED MULTI–PARTY—
MULTI–CLAIM PROCEEDINGS

A. CLASS ACTIONS

§ 8–1. General Purpose and Utility of Class Actions

The class action device allows one or more persons to sue or be sued on behalf of themselves and other individuals who allegedly possess similar grievances or have been harmed in a similar way. The action is permitted to be brought in a representative fashion in order to allow the assertion of legal rights in situations in which the numbers of people involved and, in some instances, the small individual amounts involved, otherwise effectively would prevent the vindication of those rights. Further, the device is an efficient and economical means for the courts and the parties to try a case in which there are common interests. Thus, class suits serve several important objectives.

Current opinion is divided as to the actual utility of class actions. Critics point to the fact that many of the suits filed have been extremely burdensome, costly and time-consuming, and only a few have reached judgment. Further, during the early 1970s class action filings increased to such an extent that it was argued that they have become strike suits, filed by attorneys seeking fat fees but producing few other real benefits. Although class action filings decreased in the 1980s, the 1990s have seen an upsurge in nationwide consumer and product liability class actions and critics again have charged that these suits are unmanageable and only filed to force early settlements including large attorneys' fees. Additional criticism arises because the large, complex modern class suit alters our concept of the adversary system. This is shown in two ways. First, the judge's role changes from a passive one to a very active one. This is necessitated by the fact that the judge must oversee the proceedings very carefully to make certain that the rights of the absent class members are being protected. The judge cannot rely on the named representative or counsel because at various points their interests may diverge from the absent class members. Additionally, the complexity of the action requires the judge to act in many instances as an administrator, devising notice schemes and methods of computing and distributing damages. The second major change produced by class actions is that they have thrust the courts into the policy arena. In the traditional two party suit, the court has little overt concern for the creation of law and the focus is on the specific, local problem before it. Class suits force the courts to deal with public policy questions, rather than leaving those issues to the executive or the legislature. The very numbers of persons involved reflect the fact that the policy or law being sued upon has peculiar public interest. Further, class actions litigants often function as private attorneys' general forcing adherence to or changes in the law by the very impact of their actions.

Undoubtedly in response to some of the criticisms and concerns being raised, several proposals for class action reforms are under active consideration. Stated generally, these proposals attempt to provide some protections to curtail the abuses and to streamline class action procedures while preserving the class remedy as an important tool to vindicate various rights. Thus, the debate on the utility of the class action continues and it is important to realize that an individual court's application of rule requirements (either narrowly or liberally) or its willingness to adopt new management procedures often is influenced by its feelings as to whether class action critics or advocates present the true situation.

§ 8–2. Types of Class Action Statutes

There are basically five types of class action statutes in the United States today. A brief look at those provisions illustrates some of the concerns relevant under each approach.

Originally, many states modeled their class action rules on the original equity rules. Class suits were permitted when joinder of all the members was not feasible and there was adequate representation of their interests. No further guidance was given to the courts. The major limitation on the availability of class action relief was that the device was authorized only in equity, which meant it was not available when damages were being sought. Today, with the merger of law and equity, states generally have abandoned this approach in favor of one of those that are described below.

Similar to the equity approach is that followed by those states having the Field Code as their procedural rules. See Cal.Civ.Proc.Code § 382. In those states the same minimum requirements of impracticable joinder and adequacy of representation apply, but class actions are available in law and in equity. Further, common questions must be shared by the class members. Courts frequently also interpret the code requirements as necessitating that there be an ascertainable class and that the class possess a community of interest. In looking at those requirements the judge essentially will consider whether the individual class members will be identifiable, at least at the damage stage, the number of common questions that exist as compared to the individual issues that will have to be litigated, and, at least to some degree, the social utility of the action. The test is a balancing one, with the court weighing the economies to be gained by allowing the action to proceed against concerns of adequacy of representation and cohesiveness of interest on the part of the class members.

Another type of class action rule is the 1938 federal provision, which, although it no longer is used in the federal courts, is followed in several states. Under that approach the same requirements of impracticable joinder, common questions and adequacy of representation are present. Additionally, the suit must fall into one of three categories, labeled by the courts as "true," "hybrid," and "spurious." In a "true" action the class members share a common and undivided interest. This means that under law they are recognized as united in interest, as for example, the partners in a limited partnership or a husband and wife in a community property state suing to protect their community interests. In a "hybrid" suit the members share an interest in the property that is the subject of the suit. Their interests need not be joint, rather the focus is on the property (typically a limited fund from which they are seeking relief). In a "spurious" action common questions alone authorize the class suit. The classification of a given lawsuit into a particular category in effect determines the binding effect of the judgment. Because of the loose connection existing in spurious suits, courts typically bind only those class members who opt into the action. In practice this means that an unsuccessful spurious class suit will bind only the named parties. If a judgment on liability is reached for the class, then the absent members may take advantage of it and enter to seek damages. Judgments in true or hybrid class suits will be binding on all the absent class members whether they are successful or not.

The most widely used class action statute is the 1966 version of Federal Rule 23, which governs in the federal courts, as well as in several states. The rule sets out requirements in the first two subdivisions, and then in the remaining three sections provides guidance to the courts on how to manage class actions. These last sections include: notice provisions, setting forth when notice is required and what should be included (23(c)(2) and (d)(2)); authority for restructuring the action by subclassing (23(c)(4)), and for allowing absent members to intervene (23(d)(3)); and provisions for approving and controlling settlements (23(e)). The focus is to encourage the development of flexible management devices and to provide the courts with some guidance in that area.

The class requirements under Federal Rule 23 also are stated pragmatically. The party seeking class certification must show that the action meets the requirements set out in 23(a) and falls within one of the three categories of 23(b). The basic requirements in (a) are the same as those just described under the 1938 rule. However, the subdivision (b) categories have been altered to provide more guidance and with the intention that all class action judgments will be binding, regardless of which type of suit is presented. Rule 23(b)(1) focuses on the possible adverse impact of a non-class judgment on the opposing party, who might be placed in an impossible position if faced with conflicting individual judgments, or on the absent class members, whose interests might be practically impaired if class action treatment were denied. Rule 23(b)(2) authorizes class suits in which injunctive or declaratory relief is appropriate on a class-wide basis. Rule 23(b)(3) allows class treatment if common questions predominate and if a class suit is the superior means of handling the controversy. This last provision is the catchall and there is considerable discretion given to the court to determine superiority. Among other things, the court may take into account whether the action appears to pose severe management problems, what alternatives exist, and whether the suit is important as a policy matter.

Because the only connection between the class members in a Rule 23(b)(3) suit is the presence of common questions, various procedures exist in the other portions of the rule to ensure that their interests are adequately protected. Notice is mandatory in these suits and individual notice must be mailed to all identifiable class members, Fed.Rule 23(c)(2). Eisen v. Carlisle & Jacquelin (S.Ct.1974). Absent class members may opt out of the suit, Fed.Rule 23(c)(3). If they do opt out, they will not be bound by the judgment; conversely, they cannot later take advantage of the judgment. Because these added protections—individual notice and the right to exclude oneself from the class—oftentimes are costly and burdensome, it is common for parties to try to fit the action within one of the first two categories of Rule 23(b) so as to avoid them.

The final category of class action statutes is represented by the New York statute, adopted in 1975, NYCPLR §§ 901–908, and by the 1976 proposed Uniform Class Action Statute, drafted by the Commissioners on Uniform State Laws and currently adopted in North Dakota and Iowa. Various bills also were proposed in Congress in the late 1970s to revise the federal scheme, though none ever were enacted. All of these share a common approach—they are long and complex and attempt to deal specifically with most of the many issues that have arisen under the present procedural rules. They provide much more detailed guidance to the courts on how to handle class suits and attempt to provide some solutions to problems with which the courts are struggling.

§ 8–3.　Jurisdiction Requirements

Class action rules are merely procedural and do not themselves confer jurisdiction on the courts. The question of how to apply the traditional rules regarding the establishment of jurisdiction in this complex setting raises special problems.

First, in federal courts, when the basis for jurisdiction is diversity, whose citizenship controls and how is the amount in controversy to be calculated? The first question is answered easily—only the citizenship of the named representative parties will be considered for purposes of determining whether diversity exists. With regard to the amount involved, the Supreme Court has ruled that the claims of the class members cannot be aggregated to meet the $50,000 requirement unless the class members are asserting a common and undivided interest in a single title or right. Zahn v. International Paper Co. (S.Ct.1973). What constitutes a joint and common interest is described earlier, see § 2–4, above. Failure to show a joint or common interest means that each class member must possess a claim exceeding the jurisdictional minimum. In practice, this rule severely restricts the ability to bring a common question damage suit in the federal courts when jurisdiction is based on diversity and individual claims are small—as, for example, in much consumer and environmental litigation.

The question involving the applicability of personal jurisdiction requirements in the class setting was addressed by the Supreme Court in 1985. Phillips Petroleum Co. v. Shutts (S.Ct.1985). The problem is important because if traditional jurisdiction requirements apply, then both the notice and the contact elements of due process would have to be satisfied for all absent class members. A court would have to find that the absent class members had such minimum contacts with the forum state that it would be consistent with notions of fair play and substantial justice for the court to enter a binding judgment on their claims. See generally §§ 2-9—2-20, above. This effectively would preclude any nationwide or multistate plaintiff class actions since it would be rare that the nonresident class members (the "victims") had any active contact with the forum state. Class action protagonists thus argued that class actions should be treated differently. They noted that the focus on forum contacts typically is designed to ensure that it is fair to require a defendant to defend "away from home," whereas there is no intention in the class setting of having the absentees appear and litigate in the forum. The purpose of the class suit is to allow their representative to sue on their behalf.

Thus, relying predominantly on Hansberry v. Lee (S.Ct.1940), it was argued that contacts were not necessary. The binding effect of class action judgments should not be determined by personal jurisdiction, but by due process, which requires only that the representatives adequately represent the nonresident members and that adequate notice be given. Application of these criteria is discussed in the next section.

In the Shutts case, the Supreme Court resolved the debate, ruling that it was not necessary for the court to obtain jurisdiction over the absent class members. Due process was satisfied because the class members in that case had been adequately represented and they had been sent individual notice with the opportunity to opt out. The failure to opt out acted almost as a form of implied consent. On its facts, Shutts easily satisfied due process concerns because so many protections for the absentee's rights existed. As is discussed in the next section, whether individual notice and the opportunity to exclude oneself from the class both are constitutional requirements for binding nonresident class members who otherwise are adequately represented remains unclear.

§ 8–4. Procedural Fairness: Adequacy of Representation, Notice, and Binding Effect

A major problem in allowing class actions has been how to accord class judgments total binding effect consistent with due process concerns of providing each person an opportunity to be heard. It is absolutely necessary for class judgments to bind even the unnamed members in order to achieve judicial economy. Thus, the Supreme Court has recognized class judgments as an exception to the traditional rule that only named parties to a suit are bound by a judgment therein. Supreme Tribe of Ben Hur v. Cauble (S.Ct.1921). There will be a failure of due process only when the procedures utilized do not ensure the adequate protection of the absent members. Hansberry v. Lee (S.Ct.1940).

The two procedures designed to meet due process requirements are an appropriate system for notifying the absent members and a careful inquiry by the court into the named representative's ability to adequately protect those interests. It is not clear whether these requirements are both necessary or if the satisfaction of one may cure a deficiency in the other. The lower courts have split on the question whether some form of notice is constitutionally compelled in all class suits. The Supreme Court's only decision in this area rested on a rule interpretation, mandating individual notice in actions under Federal Rule 23(b)(3), but not addressing actions under the other provisions. Eisen v. Carlisle & Jacquelin (S.Ct.1974). Similarly, the Court has not ruled on the question whether actual notice might result in the waiver of a class member's right later to object to inadequate representation. In Phillips Petroleum Co. v. Shutts (S.Ct.1985), discussed in the previous section, both adequate representation and individual notice were present and class members were provided an opportunity to opt out, as well, so the Court did not have to rule on whether due process could be satisfied in the absence of one of those protections. Thus, careful counsel should not overlook either requirement in order to ensure that the class judgment that is obtained will not be subject to collateral attack.

Adequacy of representation is a flexible concept embracing any matter that might influence how vigorously the named party will prosecute or defend the action on behalf of the class. Most central is the question whether the interests of the class and the representative are conflicting or antagonistic. The court also may inquire as to the competence of the attorney representing the class or the financial resources of the representatives to make certain that they can pursue the litigation to its end. Because adequacy of representation is so important, the court is obliged to consider that question throughout the course of the suit, not just at the certification stage. However, adequacy problems need not always result in a dismissal. The court can add additional representatives, redefine or subclass the action to avoid or eliminate conflicts, or appoint new counsel if that will permit the action to proceed with adequate protection for the absent members.

A serious question regarding notice is whether, in the absence of a mandatory statutory or rule requirement for notice, due process demands some form of actual or individual notice, where feasible, or if alternative constructive or substitute notice schemes may suffice. The constitutional standards for notice spring from a non-class suit, Mullane v. Central Hanover Bank & Trust Co. (S.Ct.1950). Although that case required mailed notice to all persons whose addresses were readily available, that conclusion rested on a finding that individual notice was feasible—not too costly or burdensome—and the Court seemed more generally to be adopting a "reasonableness" test for notice in future actions. (See § 2–21, above.) Further, there is the practical problem of what to include in the notice so as to make it meaningful to the recipient. In short, what notice is appropriate must be decided on a case by case basis, taking into account Mullane and the desire to reach as many absent class members as possible.

Finally, it has been argued that, at least in damage class actions, due process requires that nonresident absentee class members be provided an opportunity to opt out. This argument rests on the fact that when the Supreme Court upheld the Kansas scheme in Phillips Petroleum Co. v. Shutts (S.Ct. 1985) it noted as one of the protections provided that the class members had been given that opportunity. However, as is true with regard to the notice and adequate representation requirements, it remains unclear whether all of the safeguards existing in Shutts must be available in each class action to ensure its binding effect or whether a more flexible approach might be taken.

§ 8–5. Two Problems: Damage Assessment and Attorney Fees

A wide variety of problems have surfaced in the class action field. Two of the more important issues will be mentioned here: damage assessment and attorney's fees.

One of the biggest difficulties in the damage class suit is how to assess and distribute the remedy when the individual class members' claims are very small or the class is extremely large or it is potentially difficult to identify individual members. Different approaches have been tried, although all of them are controversial and not widely adopted. In some cases the courts have assessed lump sum damages based on the defendants' records, which reveal illegal profits or overcharges. This alleviates the need for individual damage trials and distribution can be done through a less costly and burdensome method—perhaps even administered by the attorneys. A few courts have gone even further and developed what is called fluid recovery for cases in which it would be extremely costly and probably futile to try to identify class members. Under that approach, after lump sum damages are proven, the court does not attempt to distribute the damages to the class members. Instead, recognizing that class suits are in the public interest, the court devises a means by which the damages can be distributed to benefit a comparable segment of the public and yet require little court supervision. For example, in a case in which a taxicab company was found to have overcharged, it was ordered to reduce fares for a certain period of time until it had disgorged the illegal profits. Daar v. Yellow Cab Co. (Cal.1967). The Second Circuit has rejected this approach on the ground that it is unauthorized by the rules and violates the defendant's due process right to be confronted by its accusers. Eisen v. Carlisle & Jacquelin (2d Cir.1973). And most federal courts have followed suit. However, the fluid recovery device remains a viable one in the state courts.

Additional problems of assessing damages exist when they cannot be calculated with reference to the defendant's records, but require inquiry into the individual class member's losses. Such individual inquiries in large class suits could result in thousands of minitrials, undercutting the judicial economy of the class action and, in some instances, creating management nightmares. In response, a few courts have experimented with allowing proof of damages based on statistical sampling and other similar devices. But these approaches have been challenged as violating the defendant's jury trial rights. Whether ultimately these challenges will be sustained by the appellate courts remains to be seen and has important implications for the future viability of damage class actions.

Another serious source of dispute in the class action field is attorney's fees. Class opponents have argued that class suits are being brought not to vindicate the public interest, but to generate large fees. In many instances this allegation appears unfortunately true. Thus, the courts have devoted considerable attention to developing and refining standards for assessing fees in order to keep fees within reasonable limits. Further, judges are particularly sensitive when reviewing proposed class action settlements that include attorney fees to ensure that the amount recovered by the class is appropriate, particularly in light of the proposed fees. The objective is to set an award that will act as an incentive to attorneys, but not result in a windfall. The amount of time spent remains the lodestar on which fees are based, although the courts are requiring much more detailed records reflecting the time spent on each aspect of preparation. This base amount then may be enhanced depending on the novel character and complexity of the case, and the perceived benefit produced by it. The amount may be reduced if the court finds that the attorneys proceeded inefficiently or to eliminate time spent on issues on which the class did not prevail. The inquiry on attorney fees thus is necessarily a detailed and complex one.

B. INTERPLEADER

§ 8–6. History and General Requirements

Interpleader is an equitable device by which a person who admits an obligation (the stakeholder) but is unsure to whom it is owed deposits the money or property with the court and serves notice on the possible claimants that they can dispute ownership among themselves. The action proceeds in two stages. First, the court determines if the use of interpleader is proper. If so, the stakeholder is dismissed from the suit. Second, the court will determine the rights to the property. Those persons served with fair notice and given an opportunity to litigate are bound both against the stakeholder and among themselves. In this way, the procedure acts to reduce multiple litigation and to protect the stakeholder from double or multiple liability or even the threat of it.

Historically, in order to utilize interpleader the stakeholder had to show that he legitimately feared multiple vexation by adverse claimants. The claimants need not be asserting ownership based on the same right, but they had to be claiming exactly the same property. Further, the stakeholder had to allege that he was not independently liable to any of the claimants on some other claims and that he was disinterested in the current stake and did not assert any claim or defense with regard to it. Modern interpleader statutes have largely abandoned these last two requirements and only multiple vexation still needs to be shown.

Other equitable restrictions may prevent interpleader, however. For example, if the stakeholder has been guilty of laches or contributed to the development of the adverse claims, the court may exercise its discretion to deny the relief. Another limitation that may prevent the use of interpleader in the state courts is that the Supreme Court has ruled that an interpleader action is in personam and that it is necessary for the court to obtain personal jurisdiction over each of the claimants in order to bind them to the decree. New York Life

Ins. Co. v. Dunlevy (S.Ct.1916). Most states have not adopted long-arm statutes to meet this requirement. (See §§ 2–9–2–10, above.) Thus, interpleader is predominantly a federal device.

§ 8–7. Federal Statutory and Rule Interpleader Compared

There are two different means of invoking interpleader in the federal courts: one is Federal Rule 22; the other is by statute, 28 U.S.C.A. § 1335. Both procedures share some similarities. There are no requirements that the stakeholder be disinterested or not be subject to independent liability. Under the rule, the stakeholder must show that he may be subject to "multiple liability." The statute refers to "multiple vexation." The courts have interpreted both phrases in the same way so that a showing of the threat of multiple suits will suffice under either provision. Further, the stakeholder may invoke either procedure on the basis of the possibility of future claims against the property; he need not wait until claims have been filed before bringing suit.

Some major differences between rule and statutory interpleader do exist, however. To begin with, different jurisdiction and venue requirements are applicable to each method. Rule 22 functions like all other joinder rules—actions utilizing it must meet normal jurisdiction and venue requirements. Statutory interpleader has special standards that apply. Thus, in a Rule 22 case, more than $50,000 must be at issue and there must be complete diversity, no claimant may share the same citizenship with the stakeholder. Minimal diversity applies in statutory interpleader and the stakeholder's citizenship is irrelevant. The only concern is that diversity exist between at least two of the claimants. State Farm Fire & Cas. Co. v. Tashire (S.Ct.1967). Further, only $500 need be involved. 28 U.S.C.A. § 1335. Personal jurisdiction over the claimants in a Rule 22 case is restricted to that which is authorized under the state law in which the court is sitting. Although Federal Rule 4 authorizes the federal courts to use state long-arm statutes to go outside the borders, most such statutes do not fit the interpleader situation because they are premised on the nonresident conducting some activity in the state, not simply being a claimant to funds deposited in the state. Thus, a Rule 22 action typically is territorially restricted—all the claimants must reside in the forum state. In contrast, nationwide service of process is available in statutory interpleader actions. 28 U.S.C.A. § 2361. Finally, venue in Rule 22 actions is proper under the general venue statute where any claimant resides, if all claimants reside in the same state, where a substantial part of the events or omissions giving use to the claim occurred (potentially difficult places to locate in this context), or where all the claimants are subject to personal jurisdiction, if no other district exists where suit may be brought. 28 U.S.C.A. § 1391. In actions under the interpleader statute, venue may be laid where any claimant resides. 28 U.S.C.A. § 1397.

Two other differences also bear mention. In statutory interpleader actions the stakeholder must deposit the property in issue with the court or post a bond for its value when suit is filed. 28 U.S.C.A. § 1335. There is no deposit requirement under Rule 22, although the court may allow the stakeholder to do so if he so desires. Fed.Rule 67. Thus, in cases in which the stakeholder would prefer to maintain control over the property as long as possible, Rule 22 interpleader provides the better alternative. On the other hand, the court is given specific authority in the statutory proceedings to enjoin the claimants from suits elsewhere. 28 U.S.C.A. § 2361. Although this power cannot be used indiscriminately to enjoin all related litigation, it does provide a potent weapon to protect the stakeholder from the harassment of multiple suits. The injunctive power of the federal court in actions under Rule 22 is less clear, because the federal anti-injunction statute, 28 U.S.C.A. § 2283, generally prohibits the federal courts from enjoining state proceedings in the absence of specific statutory authority. The only possible applicable exception would be if the interpleader court would consider an injunction in this context as "in aid of its jurisdiction." This possibility is by no means certain so that the court's injunction power may be narrower in a Rule 22 action than in a statutory action.

§ 8–8. Assertion of Additional Claims

One troublesome question that has arisen in interpleader suits is whether, once it is clear that interpleader is proper, the claimants may assert additional claims against one another or against the stakeholder. For example, if an automobile insurer interpleads its insured and several persons allegedly harmed by the insured, can those persons then assert their tort claims against one another in that action? Clearly, any additional claims would need to present independent bases of subject-matter and personal jurisdiction. This is particularly so if the claimants are properly before the court only because of the availability of nationwide service of process or minimal diversity. To hold otherwise would create an incredible burden on the claimants and is unjustified by notions of judicial economy alone. Indeed, even if there are no jurisdictional problems regarding the additional claims, it may be questioned whether allowing those claims would unduly complicate or delay the interpleader action and thus whether it is appropriate to inject those new issues into the action. The court will decide that question on a case-by-case basis.

C. MULTIDISTRICT LITIGATION

§ 8–9. Modern Techniques for Handling

A modern legal phenomenon has been the concept of mass injury. The nationwide distribution of a single defective product may harm millions of users; the single act of a nationwide business may affect hundreds or thousands of consumers; a potential securities irregularity may impact on hundreds of thousands of investors; or an air crash will injure, often kill, hundreds of passengers. The result of these mass injuries frequently has been the filing of as many lawsuits in courts around the country where the injured parties reside. Thus, considerable attention has been given to ways in which to manage these suits so as to achieve judicial economy while promoting fairness to all concerned.

It is beyond the scope of this Nutshell to inquire in detail into the various techniques that have been utilized. However, two major developments bear mention. The first is the Manual for Complex Litigation Third (1995), produced by the Federal Judicial Center and designed to highlight several problem areas in complex litigation and provide some solutions. It contains important suggestions regarding case management and the scheduling of discovery and the pretrial process, discussions of some major issues that have occurred in the class action context, citations to the recent cases dealing with these issues, and many other useful aids for the courts and attorneys involved in those suits.

The second development worth noting is statutory. A 1970 amendment to the Judicial Code established the Judicial Panel on Multidistrict Litigation. See 28 U.S.C.A. § 1407. Comprised of seven judges designated from districts around the country, the Panel is authorized upon application of any party to transfer to one district for coordinated pretrial proceedings all related actions filed in the federal courts. To obtain a transfer the movant must show that the cases share common questions of fact and that transfer will serve the "convenience of parties and witnesses" thereby promoting "the just and efficient conduct" of the actions. By this management device, duplicative discovery and pretrial motion practice is eliminated. Further, the careful selection of the transferee court produces great efficiency by relieving heavily crowded dockets of these cases, as well as assuring the parties relatively prompt action in the transferee court. Under the statute, the actions are to return to their original forums for trial. However, practice indicates that most transferee courts retain the cases until judgment is reached or the actions are settled or decided on motion so they never return, thereby further increasing the judicial economies achieved. Because of the utility of this multidistrict transfer device, serious proposals are being made for expanding its scope to allow for greater consolidation of cases dispersed in multiple fora for pretrial and trial.

CHAPTER IX

OTHER SPECIAL PROBLEMS IN FEDERAL LITIGATION

A. ACCESS BARRIERS

§ 9-1. Standing, Mootness, and Justiciability

The constitutional provision authorizing the establishment of the system of federal courts specifically extends their judicial power only to "cases" or "controversies." Art. III, § 2, U.S. Constitution. Federal courts cannot render purely advisory opinions. The problem of ascertaining what constitutes a valid case or controversy is highly complex and is studied in more detail in courses and books on federal courts or federal jurisdiction. See C. Wright, *Law of Federal Courts* 60–94 (5th ed.1994). The primary doctrines that have been developed in order to apply the Article III, § 2 requirements are those of standing, mootness, and justiciability. A brief introduction follows.

To bring a properly cognizable action in the federal courts, the plaintiff must have standing—the claimant must have suffered a direct or actual injury, as opposed to a more general injury. Questions regarding standing arise most commonly when a plaintiff attempts to challenge a statute or some aspect of governmental decisionmaking. The presence of an actual injury ensures that the questions raised in the suit are not merely hypothetical and that they are being presented in an adversary context comprising a "case." Further, requiring an actual injury ensures that the plaintiff has a sufficient stake in the outcome that he will pursue the action to the fullest. Plaintiffs aggrieved at public spending cannot file suit against the government solely on the ground that they are taxpayers and are affected thereby. There is no direct injury and standing is not available.

Although standing restrictions spring from the constitutional requirement that federal courts entertain only cases or controversies, decisions in particular cases also may involve serious policy considerations, sometimes referred to as the "prudential" aspects of standing. This feature makes it very difficult to reconcile various decisions because the court in each case is deciding not only whether the claimant was in fact injured, but also whether the issues involved are such that the legislature should be allowed to carry out its policies without judicial interference. Thus, standing requirements serve as a control on the types of issues that may be decided by the courts.

Mootness addresses the same basic question as standing: does the plaintiff have a live or real case. The main difference is the time at which mootness issues are raised. Standing is addressed at the outset of the action. But the plaintiff must continue to suffer actual injury throughout the course of the litigation in order to meet the case or controversy requirement. If he does not, the action is said to be moot and will be dismissed. For example, a prisoner suing to challenge visitation regulations may have standing at the outset. However, if the prisoner is paroled or if the regulations are changed before the case reaches judgment, his claim is no longer live and the action may be dismissed for mootness. In this way the federal courts are protected from rendering advisory opinions on hypothetical questions.

Justiciability focuses on the issues being raised, rather than the claimant. An issue may be held non-justiciable because it is not yet ripe for review or because the court concludes that it involves essentially a political decision, rather than a judicial one. Thus, the concept of justiciability is very fluid. The courts invoke it whenever for some reason they conclude that the issues presented in an action should not be decided at that time. The rationale utilized is that those issues do not comprise a controversy of the type envisioned by the drafters of the Constitution.

B. WHAT LAW GOVERNS

§ 9–2. The Erie Doctrine

The question of what law governs in a federal court sitting in a case that is not based on a specific federal law (most commonly, courts sitting in diversity) has posed one of the most difficult problems in federal court litigation. It goes to the heart of the relationship between the federal and state governments. It is a problem studied intensively in advanced courses in conflicts or federal jurisdiction. A more detailed treatment may be found in J. Friedenthal, M. Kane & A. Miller, *Civil Procedure* Ch. 4 (2d ed.1993).

Until 1938, the balance was tipped in favor of federal control and the federal courts asserted the power to create general federal common law. This position derived from the Supreme Court's interpretation of the Rules of Decision Act, 28 U.S.C.A. § 1652, in Swift v. Tyson (S.Ct.1842). The Act specifically requires that except when the Constitution, treaties or an Act of Congress otherwise provides, the federal courts shall apply the "laws of the several states" as the rules of decision in their courts. The Swift Court interpreted the reference to "laws" in the statute as being limited to state statutes or to state common law on issues peculiarly "local" in character. Then, in Erie R. Co. v. Tompkins (S.Ct.1938), the Court overruled Swift, holding that "laws" in the Rules of Decision Act includes judge-made law, and returning the power to develop common law to the states. The Supreme Court has carefully elucidated the kind of analysis necessary to decide whether federal or state law should govern on particular issues when a federal court is sitting in diversity jurisdiction in a series of decisions since 1938 and the study of this entire line of cases is referred to as the Erie doctrine.

There are two situations that must be distinguished. The first is when the federal court is deciding whether it has the authority to create common law on a particular issue. The second requires the federal court to decide whether it must follow state law even though there is a federal rule of civil procedure that appears applicable. In the first case, Erie makes it clear that federal courts have no power to create a body of general federal common law to govern substantive rights; that is a power reserved to the states under the Tenth Amendment. The only constitutional interpretation of the Rules of Decision Act is that state law, whether in statutory or common law form, governs on matters substantive.

When a federal rule is involved, however, the federal government has a legitimate interest because part of the process of establishing a federal court system as authorized by the United States Constitution (Art. III, § 2) includes prescribing procedural rules to regulate the court system. The Congress has recognized this need and, utilizing its authority under the Necessary and Proper Clause (Art. I, § 8) has enacted the Rules Enabling Act, 28 U.S.C.A. § 2072, authorizing the Supreme Court to promulgate rules of procedure for the federal courts. The Supreme Court has used this authority to develop the current Federal Rules of Civil Procedure. Thus, if the court is confronted with a question whether state law must be applied when a seemingly applicable Federal Rule exists, the Rules of Decision Act is no longer apposite. The proper question is whether the rule is within the scope of the Rules Enabling Act. The answer requires an inquiry into whether the rule actually is designed to regulate the processes of the courts or whether it will alter the rules of decision by which the court will adjudicate the merits of the dispute. If the former is so, the statutory and constitutional standards are met and the federal rule should control. Hanna v. Plumer (S.Ct.1965).

This description presents the two ends of the spectrum. In many instances the law or issue involved cannot be classified as purely substantive or the federal rule in question may not speak directly to the question involved. The proper analysis to determine whether the federal court is bound to apply state law under these circumstances was suggested in the Hanna case. It would proceed as follows.

The first step is to ascertain whether there is a federal rule applicable to the issue. If not, then consider the following four factors. One: is the issue one which is tightly or loosely bound up with the creation of the rights being sued upon? Stated alternatively, how substantive is the state's law? Two: would the application of a different rule by the federal court be outcome determinative in the sense that it would produce forum shopping in favor of the federal courts or would result in the unequal administration of the law? For example, the application of different limitations periods in federal and state courts on the same causes of action would be very outcome determinative. Guaranty Trust Co. v. York (S.Ct.1945). Three: what is the federal interest in avoiding the state law or the federal policy to be fostered by applying federal law? Four:

would the use of a federal standard have an adverse impact on federalism (would it intrude on the state's ability to regulate a legitimate area of state interest)? Byrd v. Blue Ridge Rural Elec. Cooperative, Inc. (S.Ct.1958). In balancing these four factors, the court in close cases will take into account that the thrust of the Erie doctrine is to defer to the states unless some important federal interest is involved or the application of federal law to the issue presented will interfere with the state's regulatory interest.

If there is a federal rule that addresses the issue involved, then the second step is to decide whether there is a conflict between the state and federal rules. If no conflict exists, then the inquiry is the same as just outlined above—is the federal court required to consider applying state law under the Rules of Decision Act—and the same four part balancing test applies. For example, if the federal rule does not speak specifically to the issue posed, but only generally regulates the area, and the state rule presents a very specific requirement not inconsistent with that regulation, then there is no conflict because the court could apply the state law without violating the federal provision. Cohen v. Beneficial Indus. Loan Corp. (S.Ct.1949). Similarly, even if the two rules appear to conflict on their face, if the federal and state rules are designed for different purposes, then both can be applied if, after balancing the four factors, it appears that the federal court ought to defer to state law. Walker v. Armco Steel Corp. (S.Ct.1980). However, if the federal rule conflicts with the state law, then the inquiry becomes whether the federal rule was properly promulgated within the scope of the Rules Enabling Act, as described above. If it is proper, the Supremacy Clause, Art. VI, mandates that it control. A conflict may be found, for example, if the federal rule is discretionary, but the state rule sets out mandatory requirements because the notion of mandatory requisites would be inconsistent with the federal court's ability to exercise its discretion and decide each case in relation to its facts. Burlington Northern R. Co. v. Woods (S.Ct.1987). If the court determines that a particular federal rule is not within the enabling legislation, then it again must refer to the four part analysis described above in order to determine whether it yet must follow the state law under the Rules of Decision Act. To date, no federal rule has been found to violate the Rules Enabling Act; therefore, as a practical matter, once the rules are found to be in conflict, the federal rule governs. However, consistent with the general policy underlying Erie, the federal courts often will strain to find that the rules are not in conflict so as to be able to defer to the state provision when no strong federal interest is involved.

A similar analysis is used when the question presented is whether a federal statute, rather than a federal rule of civil procedure, or state law should control a particular issue. The courts will look to see whether the statute in fact was designed to address the issue presented and whether it is in conflict with the way in which state law handles the issue. If the answer to those two questions is yes, the federal statute governs under the Supremacy Clause, Art. VI. See Stewart Organization, Inc. v. Ricoh Corp. (S.Ct.1988). If the statute does not cover the issue or is not in conflict, then the court must ascertain whether it nonetheless must defer to state law under the Rules of Decision Act by balancing the four factors described above.

Throughout this discussion the assumption has been that the federal court easily can ascertain the existing state law on a given issue in order to do the kind of balancing of policies described. Unfortunately, this is not always so. It is not uncommon for the federal court to be faced with a situation in which state law is in flux with no recent ruling by the state supreme court or in which local rulings may not exist on the question. In those circumstances the federal judge must attempt to determine the law that she believes the state court would follow if it were ruling on the issue; she cannot simply apply the law she decides is "best."

§ 9–3. Choosing Which State's Law Controls

The question whether a federal court is bound by state law is only one of the governing law questions confronting a federal diversity court. In cases in which parties and events cross state lines, the court also must determine which state's law should control. The principles governing state-to-state choice of law decisions are taught in courses in Conflict of Laws and are outside the scope of this volume.

Suffice it to note here that no single set of choice of law principles prevails; instead various theories exist, with different states following separate approaches to this problem.

Because of the lack of coherence in choice of law doctrine, a significant issue is posed in federal diversity cases as to whether the federal court can decide to apply a federal conception of conflict of laws rules or must look to state choice of law rules for guidance. The Supreme Court answered this question in Klaxon Co. v. Stentor Elec. Manufacturing Co. (S.Ct.1941), ruling that the principle of vertical uniformity between the federal and state courts promoted by Erie R.R. Co. v. Tompkins (see § 9–2, above) requires the federal courts to apply the forum state's choice of law rules in order to determine which state's law controls. Although this result reduces the potential for forum shopping between federal and state courts, it necessarily encourages forum shopping between federal courts in order to lodge suit in the court in the state whose conflict of laws principles will best serve the interests of the plaintiff. Nonetheless, the Klaxon rule remains controlling today.

Forum shopping between federal courts in different states is encouraged further because of the rules applicable to choosing between competing state laws when cases are transferred from one federal court to another. (See § 2–30, above). The transferee court must apply the choice of law rules of the original transferor forum. Van Dusen v. Barrack (S.Ct.1964). A transfer changes the courtroom, not the law. However, the plaintiff's original forum selection must be proper and not arbitrary. If the case is transferred because of improper venue, then the transferee court can apply the choice of law rules of its own state.

§ 9–4. Federal Common Law

Erie R. Co. v. Tompkins did not remove all authority from the federal courts to create common law. It only restricted that power in circumstances in which the court is sitting in diversity and no clear federal statutory or constitutional interest pertains so that the Rules of Decision Act mandates that state law govern. The source of authority for the creation of federal common law may be an explicit or implicit statutory grant or, in some instances, it may derive from the Constitution itself. There is no consistent or persistent practice. A few examples suggest the extent of the federal courts' power.

A most vivid example of a Congressional grant of common law power is Federal Rule of Evidence 501, enacted in 1976. In that rule the federal courts are instructed to apply to federal cases "the [privilege] rules of the courts of the United States as developed in the light of reason and experience." An implied congressional directive was found in the labor field when the Supreme Court ruled that when Congress placed special labor law jurisdiction in the federal courts it impliedly authorized them to develop a uniform, national law of collective bargaining, unfettered by what the states might do. Textile Workers Union v. Lincoln Mills (S.Ct.1957). Constitutional, as opposed to statutory, authority to create common law has been found in the international relations field, Banco Nacional de Cuba v. Sabbatino (S.Ct.1964), on questions of apportioning interstate waters, Hinderlider v. La Plata River & Cherry Creek Ditch Co. (S.Ct.1938), and in cases defining the obligations of the United States government on federal commercial paper, Clearfield Trust Co. v. United States (S.Ct.1943).

The distinction between these cases upholding federal common law authority and the Erie case itself is one relating to the degree of federal interest. The grant of diversity jurisdiction in Article III, § 2, does not alone establish a federal regulatory interest, it merely reflects a desire to provide an impartial forum for out-of-state residents who might feel prejudiced in local fora. When there is a direct federal interest involved, such as those described in the preceding paragraph, the Tenth Amendment no longer controls and the courts may feel free to create common law in order to implement or protect that interest. Further, once a decision has been made that it is appropriate to create federal common law on a particular issue or in a particular field, that law displaces state statutory as well as decisional law by virtue of the Supremacy Clause, Art. VI, and, as is discussed in the next section, it must be applied by both federal and state courts.

§ 9–5. Federal Law in State Courts

When an action based on a federal statute is brought in state court, the court is faced with a governing law question for any matter that is not explicitly provided for in the federal statute. Can the state court utilize its own procedures and develop common law on the issue or must it be bound by the approach or law developed in the federal courts? While the statement of the problem appears the same as that confronting the federal diversity court, its resolution is somewhat different. The rationale supporting the Erie doctrine is based on the Tenth Amendment's reservation of power to the states. That requires the difficult analysis of whether there is some federal interest that would place the case outside the reserve clause. When the action is in state court, however, the Supremacy Clause of the Constitution requires those courts to follow federal law—no careful balancing of interests is necessary.

In order not to place too great a burden on state courts having concurrent jurisdiction, the Supreme Court has ruled that the state may utilize its own procedures for trying the case, however. The key is that those procedures must be applied nondiscriminatorily to state and federal cases, Testa v. Katt (S.Ct.1947), and they cannot impinge on the federal substantive rights being asserted. Dice v. Akron, Canton & Youngstown R. Co. (S.Ct.1952). The state courts are not required to adopt an entire new superstructure in order to try federal actions.

*

INDEX

---

*